A HISTORY OF THE

HOTEL GALVEZ

KATHLEEN MACA

THE
History
PRESS

Published by The History Press
Charleston, SC
www.historypress.com

Front cover: author's collection.
Back cover: Galveston Texas History Center at Rosenberg Library, Galveston, Texas; *inset*: Galveston Texas History Center at Rosenberg Library, Galveston, Texas.

Unless otherwise noted, all images are courtesy of the Galveston Texas History Center at Rosenberg Library, Galveston, Texas.

First published 2021

Manufactured in the United States

ISBN 9781625858443

Library of Congress Control Number: 2020945794

This book is dedicated to my mother, Patte Marlene Scott Shanahan, who passed away from Alzheimer's while I was writing this book. Her love of people, history, antiques, old buildings and the beach lives in every story I share about Galveston.

CONTENTS

CONTENTS

ACKNOWLEDGEMENTS

I would like to acknowledge the staff of Rosenberg Library's Galveston Texas History Center for their support during the research process: Special Collections Manager Lauren Martino, Archivist Kevin Kinney and especially Senior Archivist Sean McConnell (bless your patient heart!). I also thank Sharon Gillins for her help with obtaining photos from the Moody Family Collections.

Unless otherwise noted, all images are courtesy of the Galveston Texas History Center at Rosenberg Library, Galveston, Texas.

INTRODUCTION

Included in the National Register of Historic Places, Hotel Galvez, known as the "Queen of the Gulf," has reigned over Galveston's famous seawall for more than a century.

It began as the vision of a group of determined businessmen to bring prosperity and tourism back to their island after the 1900 Storm, the deadliest natural disaster in American history.

Victorians have sauntered down its Peacock Alley in their best finery, beauty pageant contestants have posed on its lawn, the U.S. Coast Guard has used it as a barracks and generations of families have come to love it as a holiday escape. Its guests have included presidents, celebrities, members of the military and some even say ghosts.

Come walk the halls of the Hotel Galvez with us and travel through the history of one America's most beautiful and historic hotels.

1

THE FIRST GRAND BEACH HOTEL

The Hotel Galvez was not the first grand beachfront hotel on Galveston Island. That honor belongs to the impressive Beach Hotel, designed by famed architect Nicholas Clayton.

During much of the nineteenth century, Galveston was Texas's largest city, known as the "Queen City of the Gulf." The prosperity of the city resulted in grand homes and lavish entertainments. Combined with the tropical climate, these attractions enticed numerous tourists to the island.

The Beach Hotel held its grand opening on July 4, 1883, in answer to a call for a waterfront hotel befitting a community of such wealth.

The massive Victorian structure was built directly on the beach between Twenty-Third and Twenty-Fifth Streets atop three hundred cedar pilings anchored in the sand. A central tower and a highly articulated red-and-white-striped roof topped the four-story wood frame hotel, which was painted in various shades of green. Each guest room featured a large window, and wide porches circled the structure.

Advertisements in the *Galveston Daily News* in August 1884 announced the addition of a menagerie to the grounds for the purpose of amusing hotel guests. Large metal cages beneath the hotel's front stairs held Mexican lions (mountain lions), panthers, exotic birds and other wildlife. This type of menagerie was a predecessor of modern zoos but without the educated care for the animals' welfare expected today. The welfare of guests was endangered as well, and one of the caged panthers mauled a boy the following November. This prompted a $15,000 lawsuit by the child's father against the Beach Hotel Company and quite a bit of negative press.

Many of the inhabitants of the menagerie were lost during the hurricane of August 20, 1886, with the exception of two Mexican lions, who escaped. The ferocious creatures were hunted and killed, but not before the tracking party accidentally shot one of their own members.

The Beach Hotel never again kept a menagerie.

Financial difficulties caused the hotel to close in 1895, and the structure fell into disrepair. It was sold and renovated in 1896, but bankruptcy soon followed. After being sold one more time, the Beach Hotel was shut down by city officials, who discovered that waste from the property was being emptied into the Gulf rather than the sewage lines.

On July 22, 1898, Beach Hotel proprietor George Korst completed preparations for the reopening of the property to guests. The storeroom was filled with groceries, the bar was stocked with liquor and eighty dollars in silver had been put in the safe to use for change the following day.

The staff finished their evening meal at 6:00 p.m. and threw buckets of water across the kitchen floor to clean it. The soaked wood floor would remain wet through the night as the water slowly drained through the crevices and the boards dried.

Korst had done a check of the lights on the property at 10:00 p.m., and hotel watchman Frank Lorenzo was awake until 11:00 p.m. Everything was in order to receive guests the next morning.

One guest, a Mr. Fass, had checked in early and was staying in a southwest corner room on the first floor, but it was not destined to be a restful night. Around 4:30 a.m. on July 23, a mysterious fire began in the boiler room of the Beach Hotel. Moses Harris, a clerk with the Santa Fe Railway whose Avenue Q home faced the rear of the big hotel, spotted the blaze from his bedroom window. Having no telephone, he stepped onto his porch with a pistol and fired several shots to sound an alarm.

A proofreader for the *Galveston News* named William Rice lived two blocks from the Beach Hotel and claimed to see the flames coming from the boiler room, smell kerosene oil and witness a man running from the property.

The home of Galveston Brewing employee Louis Grelling was one block west of the structure. When his wife woke him to alert him to the fire, they rushed to their bedroom window to see a blaze the size of a barn door burning at the base of the hotel. Grelling called the fire department after discovering that his own home was already blistering from the heat, but due to weak pressure at the fireplug, water was unable to reach even his front porch.

Lorenzo, who had lived at the hotel since it closed the previous summer, was using the first-floor office as his sleeping quarters. Awakened by smoke, he set off alarm bells throughout the property and quickly went to Fass's room and the living apartments of sixteen employees below. The watchman went from room to room, calmly explaining that the boiler room was on fire. Although there was most likely no danger, everyone was asked to evacuate as soon as they were able.

Fass, who had been asleep, hurriedly dressed but took the time to pack most of his belongings in a trunk and demanded that an attendant take it outside.

Fire Chief Ernest P. Wegner and his men focused most of their energy on saving surrounding structures threatened by the heat and flying embers, realizing it was too late to save the hotel. It had long been understood that if fire got underway at the large wood structure, it would burn like tinder.

The inferno was so intense that one hundred feet of fire department hose burned. Firemen had to keep their clothes wet while battling the flames.

The spectacle of the immense fire drew a crowd of onlookers, who police kept at a safe distance by roping off the area. Police also helped merchants and residents remove their belongings from the endangered surrounding buildings and warded off early looters.

A small seashell-and-curio shop owned by Francis Kraus at the corner of Twenty-Fourth and Beach burned to the ground after sparks flew from the hotel. His son, who had been sleeping in the shop at the time, managed to

Rare image taken before the seawall was built, showing Kraus's shell shop and island grade level with shore, circa 1900. *Author's collection.*

save about one-third of the merchandise before policemen pulled him from the building, overcome with heat and smoke.

Next door to the shell shop, a restaurant owned by immigrant T. Pacillo suffered the same fate, and a Ferris wheel in the area was destroyed.

Firemen focused streams of water on the nearby Julian's Place Restaurant and Saloon, the Lassaigne Hotel and Klondike Saloon and succeeded in saving them.

The tiny home belonging to a poor family at the corner of the Galveston Ball Park between Twenty-Second and Twenty-Third Streets burned to ashes, along with their few possessions.

Telegraph, telephone and electric light poles caught fire, and even the wood blocks in the street pavement and surrounding streetcar tracks were damaged. By 6:00 p.m., the massive dome of the hotel had collapsed and the hotel had dissolved into ashes.

Korst was convinced that the fire was the work of an arsonist. The kitchen floor, still thoroughly soaked from earlier that night, would have been impossible to set ablaze without the help of an accelerant.

Two nights before the calamity, in the same early hours, a small fire set with coal oil in the boiler room had been discovered in time to be extinguished.

Suspiciously, the Beach Hotel had been uninsured from May 1897 until the Monday preceding the weekend fire, when the owners took out a $25,000 policy.

Just fifteen years after the exquisite Beach Hotel opened, it lay in smoking ruins on the sand. Had the fire taken place one week later, the hotel would have been filled with visitors.

1900 STORM

The most dramatic event in the story of Galveston Island revolves around the 1900 Storm, a devastating hurricane that still stands as the deadliest natural disaster in the history of the United States. At the end of the nineteenth century, Galveston was home to over thirty-seven thousand people and was a thriving shipping, banking and commercial center known as the "Wall Street of the West." Trains carried cargo to and from the port, where one thousand ships docked annually. More than 70 percent of the country's cotton crop passed through the port.

The commerce created a prosperous community with elegant Victorian homes, hotels and theaters. It was known for many "firsts" in Texas, including the state's first medical and nursing schools, insurance company, electric power plant, country club and golf course, post office, customs house and telephones. An idyllic vacation destination, wealthy travelers from around the country visited the island to see its grandeur and bathe in the warm waters of the Gulf.

In the days before hurricanes were assigned names by the U.S. Weather Bureau, they were identified by the year they occurred. To this day, the event is known as the 1900 Storm.

Scientists in Cuba had developed some of the most successful storm-tracking systems of the era and predicted that the storm's path would take it to the Gulf of Mexico. The ten-year-old U.S. Weather Bureau, a predecessor to the National Weather Service, was not as advanced, and the bureau's director, Willis Moore, shut off the flow of data from Cuba out of professional jealousy. Moore also forbade regional forecasters from issuing their own hurricane warnings without first clearing it through the Weather Bureau offices in Washington, which was hampered by communication systems of the day.

The Weather Bureau's chief observer in Galveston, Isaac Cline, distrusted the national forecast, but by the time he was allowed to relay warnings to the community, it was too late.

On September 8, 1900 a powerful hurricane descended on the town, wiping buildings from their foundations and killing many in its path.

Scales to categorize the strength of hurricanes did not exist until seventy years after the storm, but modern meteorologists have examined information about the 1900 disaster and determine that the storm was a category 4 hurricane with winds exceeding 135 miles per hour.

In 1900, before the storm, the entire beach was level with the surf, and the highest points in the city ranged between seven to nine feet above sea level. A proposal to build a seawall in 1886 had been rejected as too expensive. Now, the citizens of Galveston would pay a high price for that decision.

The storm surge crested at fifteen feet and pushed across the island, crushing almost everything in its path. When the wind and rain stopped, the island lay in ruins. Over 3,600 buildings, two-thirds of the city, were destroyed, including the entire wharf front. Many of those still standing were badly damaged. The wagon bridge to the mainland had washed away, and the railroads were heavily impaired. Uncontrolled fires burned day and night for weeks. About thirty thousand people were left homeless, and an estimated six thousand to eight thousand people were killed— nearly a quarter of Galveston's citizens. Cline's own pregnant wife was among the victims.

To put the loss of life into context with more recent news, 1,836 people died as a result of Hurricane Katrina in 2005.

Bodies lay everywhere across the island and beneath rubble. With an imminent threat of disease, the grisly task of recovering victims took priority in the coastal heat. Though some were buried where they were found, most were taken to the Strand before being loaded onto barges, weighted and pushed overboard in the Gulf. When those bodies washed ashore days later, citizens constructed funeral pyres to burn the remains. The fires burned into November.

During the first month of cleanup following the hurricane, about seventy additional victims were discovered each day. The last body was found in February 1901. Many were never identified.

The city of Galveston would never regain its status as a financial leader, but it would succeed in rising again by reinventing itself.

While the 1900 Storm took place a decade before construction of the Hotel Galvez began, it would set the stage for a new era on the island, during which the spirit and determination of Galvestonians would become legendary.

These were the predawn hours of the "Queen of the Gulf."

BUILDING THE SEAWALL

The city of Galveston was determined to rebuild after the 1900 Storm and understood that drastic measures needed to be taken to ensure that a tragedy of that scale never happened again.

An advisory board of three engineers, known as the Robert Board, was appointed in 1901 to formulate plans for the seawall construction and grade raising. Brigadier General Henry Martyn Robert was retired from the U.S. Army and had been extensively involved in the dredging of Galveston Harbor. Alfred Noble had experience with coastal engineering projects in Chicago, including a grade raising. Henry Clay Ripley had designed one of the bridges linking Galveston Island to mainland Texas during his time with the U.S. Army Corps of Engineers.

On January 25, 1902, the board presented its recommendation for the construction of a curved-face, concrete seawall spanning three miles in length along the coastline to absorb the impact of waves as they struck the shore, as well as an elevation of the ground level of Galveston using fill dredged from the bay.

It was no small task.

The contractor for the job, J.M. O'Rourke and Company of Denver, built the wall in fifty-foot interlocking sections. A staggering 1,200 railway carloads of round, wood piles were driven forty to fifty feet deep into the beachfront and set four feet apart. Next, the crews sunk 4,000 carloads of wood sheet pilings twenty-six feet into the sea floor to protect the piles from being undermined by the waters of the Gulf.

Then, 1,000 carloads of cement were poured over the pilings, after they had been reinforced with five carloads of steel rods placed every three feet. The workmen poured an average of one hundred feet of wall each day. To protect the wall from erosion, 3,700 carloads of four-foot square granite blocks (riprap), stacked three to four feet deep, were placed from the toe of the wall, extending twenty-seven feet out into the waters.

An additional 5,200 railway carloads of crushed granite and 1,800 carloads of sand were required for the project. If it had been possible to weigh the finished product, the scale would tip at forty thousand pounds per foot of length.

The Gulf side of the seawall was concave to break the wave action and deflect waves back on themselves.

When the seventeen-foot-high wall was finished, it was sixteen feet wide at the base, five feet wide at the top and almost three-and-one-half miles long. An embankment about one hundred feet wide was built up behind the concrete wall and paved with bricks to create a thoroughfare.

Construction of the initial segment of the wall took place between 1902 and 1904, at a cost of almost $1.6 million. Westward and eastward additions

Grand opening day of the Hotel Galvez, viewed from the Galveston Boardwalk, 1911.

Crowded seawall showing Murdoch's Bathhouse with Hotel Galvez in the background. The two red granite seawall construction monuments in the foreground can still be seen today.

to the seawall were made in later years, making the wall almost ten and a half miles long today.

While the seawall was being constructed, Galveston began the enormous task of raising the elevation of approximately five hundred city blocks on the island behind it. This would not only support the wall but also facilitate drainage and sewage systems to replace problematic ones from the past.

Hand-turned jackscrews were used to raise more than 2,100 buildings as high as seventeen feet off the ground, with each worker thrusting a rotation of a screw in unison to the beat of a drum. Small houses that had withstood the storm presented little challenge, but other, more imposing structures called for engineering prowess. It took three hundred jacks to lift the exquisite brick Moody Mansion and seven hundred jacks to lift the three-thousand-ton St. Patrick's Catholic Church the necessary five feet.

A slurry of water and fill sand was dredged out of an area between the jetties at the entrance to Galveston Harbor and then pumped to discharge stations in the residential district through a canal twenty feet deep, two hundred feet wide and two and a half miles long.

Over 350 houses were temporarily relocated to provide a path for the canal to be dug. Residents used temporary catwalks to walk eight to ten feet above the sludge as the long process of drying out took place. As the water drained away and left sand behind, foundations were constructed beneath the raised structures on top of the fill. Once this was accomplished, the buildings were attached to their new bases.

In addition to buildings, sewers, streetcar tracks, water and gas lines, fire hydrants, telephone and telegraph poles, fences and outbuildings had to be lifted or repositioned. Homeowners who couldn't afford the raising process either had to sacrifice the bottom floor of their houses or abandon their homes.

Visitors to Galveston today can easily spot examples of buildings and even cemetery monuments whose lower sections were covered during the raising.

The area immediately behind the new seawall was raised just over sixteen and a half feet, with the grade slowly sloping downward going west so the city's streets drained into the bay. The project required 16.3 million cubic yards of sandy dredged fill. The work was done in quarter-mile sections for seven years, ending in 1910.

The luxurious Hotel Galvez, sitting on its beachfront seaside throne, opened one year after the barrier was finished, completing Galveston's statement of resilience to the world.

Seawall Boulevard was officially opened to automobiles at the end of the 1911 summer season, though residents had used it since the previous year. On May 25, 1912, the first causeway to the mainland also opened to vehicles, opening the gates to a new age of tourism on Galveston Island.

4

A DREAM BEGINS

O n Sunday, February 13, 1910, a group of prominent Galveston businessmen met to formulate a plan to build a resort hotel on the city's Boulevard (now known as Seawall Boulevard) and estimated that bringing this to fruition would cost approximately half a million dollars.

Isaac Herbert Kempner of I.H. Kempner Interests, John Sealy of Hutchings-Sealy & Company, Bertrand Adoue and Joseph Lobit of Adoue & Lobit and Harry Sidney Cooper of the Galveston Electric Company agreed that their firms would subscribe $50,000 each toward the project on the condition that the remainder of the amount be raised by the community. They decided that a board of directors would be elected and no salaries or bonuses would be paid, ensuring that all funds raised would go directly to the purchase of land and construction costs.

An announcement was printed in the newspaper that evening calling all members of the Galveston Business League to a meeting the following night at 8:00 p.m. in Cathedral Hall to assist in devising a plan to raise the rest of the necessary funds. After an hour of inspiring speeches and discussion behind closed doors, an astounding additional $100,000 was pledged toward the project. Although the original intent of the meeting was not to ask for subscriptions that night, the result was one of the best Valentine's Day gifts the city ever received.

It was time to open the subscription drive to the public. A member of the league stepped onto the stage of the Grand Opera House the following

COME TO GALVESTON

Via Any of These Railroads or Steamship Lines

M. K. & T.
Frisco
Santa Fe
Southern Pacific
Trinity & Brazos Valley
Galveston, Houston & Henderson
Houston & Texas Central
Missouri Pacific
St. Louis, Iron Mountain & Southern
International & Great Northern
Colorado & Southern
Cotton Belt Route
Rock Island Lines
Texas Midland
Ft. Worth & Denver City Ry.
Texas Central R. R.
Atchison, Topeka & Santa Fe
Kansas City Southern
Southern Ry.
Illinois Central R. R.
Chicago & Eastern Illinois
Chicago & Alton
Burlington Route
San Antonio & Aransas Pass
New Orleans & Pacific
Texas & Pacific
Mallory Line

But—
COME TO GALVESTON

ALONG the Gulf side of the city—the play-side—stretches the famous Sea Wall—an impregnable bulwark against tempest and tides—17 feet high, measuring 16 feet at the base and 5 feet at the top. Below it stretches the smooth, hard beach—extending either side far beyond the limits of Galveston for 30 miles. There is nothing else like this in all the world.

It is ideal weather all the time with more than 300 days of sunshine an average temperature of 70 degrees the year round and an unceasing Gulf breeze, cool in summer and warm in winter. There is absolutely no malaria. Galveston has the finest bathing beach in the world, and a straightaway automobile course of thirty miles to the end of the island, and on which can be made sixty miles with one turn, not excelled in America.

Hotel Galvez stands in a plaza of palms and oleanders, fronting the Sea Wall and looking out over the Gulf.

Hotel Galvez is a real hotel—a modern six story structure built of solid fire-proof concrete in Spanish mission architecture. It is the result of a demand for a perfect hostelry in the Southwest.

Left and next two pages: Hotel Galvez tourism brochure, circa 1918.

THE building and furnishing of this magnificent structure represents the outlay of more than a million dollars, and one may rest assured that every comfort obtainable in the best hotels of Chicago and New York have been provided here. The illustrations running through this book, while true to life, give but a vague representation of the originals. No hotel could be more complete in point of beauty of architecture, in floor arrangement, in room and suite arrangement, in the liberal space alloted to general assemblage places, in the furnishings of the building throughout.

The cuisine and dining service is under the direction of one of the most capable stewards in this country. Sea food, fresh from the water, plays no small part in the success of this department. Fish, crabs, oysters and fresh game are to be had at all times in season. The capacity of our dining quarters is 800 guests at a single meal period.

Needless to say that one can be in constant communication with the world by means of railroads, boat, mail, telegraph, stock ticker, and every other form of transfer of ideas.

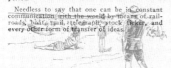

THE air of refinement pervades this entire establishment. There is not the usual hustle and bustle common to metropolitan hostelries. Celebrities, statesmen, actors and well traveled people say it is a restful place for those who would rest, a pleasureable place for those who seek excitement. Take it as you will, there is no better place to spend the winter holidays than at Hotel Galvez.

The rates at this hotel are not exorbitant. One may secure accomodations here to meet his requirements.

Guests of Hotel Galvez have the privilege of the Galveston Country Club, 18 hole Golf Course, which ranks with the best resort Golf Course in the country. The Club is 15 minutes from the hotel via automobile.

The Tarpon and deep sea fishing for Spanish Mackerel, Red Snapper and a hundred other of the finny tribe, is a lure hard to resist. The greatest Tarpon waters of the world are but ten miles from the boat landing at Galveston. A catch of two or three of these game monsters in a forenoon is a matter of daily occurance. And this is not one of the proverbial Walton stories.

THE Canvasback, the Mallard, Teal, the Redhead, the Wild Goose, and other edible water fowls migrate to this natural retreat in the Fall months and remain until Spring. The shallow water branches leading into the Gulf of Mexico offer the greatest sport in this class of outdoor life it is possible to conceive. The prairies surrounding Galveston are alive with the quail and rabbit, and one who enjoys this sport will miss much if he leaves his "shooting irons" at home.

Proud as Galveston is of her mammoth wharves, spread with acres of cotton bales and cargoes of every description, it is a lighter, more buoyant side the city turns toward the visitor. The pride of her citizens is shown in the beauty of her well-kept streets and handsome residences.

Not only unparalleled beauties of Nature adorn Galveston lavishly, but some of the greatest construction and engineering marvels of the age are to be found at Galveston—the Causeway, the $15,000,000 Jetties, the tried and tested Sea Wall

and the famous experiment in Grade Raising—now no longer an experiment.

Bathing, boating, tennis, golfing —every outdoor longing is answered by a sojourn on Galveston Island. A great deal of pleasure can be crowded into a week-end, but there is variety enough to make a long season one of endless delight for every visitor here. Nowhere is there another Galveston! The Island City is unique—an objective for every world tourist. It is known far and wide as the sportsman's paradise; home of the monster Tarpon and other game denizens of the deep.

But the sport of sports is sea-bathing, in the invigorating waters of the Gulf of Mexico, on the hard smooth beach, which has made Galveston famous. Here is admittedly the finest surf-bathing to be found anywhere in the world.

There is no treacherous undertow, but the gentle sloping beach insures security. Here the invalid gathers health and strength, and long hours are swiftly sped watching the gay crowds on the beach, and the frolics of the breakers. Thanks to

the warming Gulf Stream there is always good bathing at Galveston and the season is at its height, of course, from the end of March to November.

Could you find anywhere in the world a spot more delightful for your Winter or Summer playground—or one answering your sportsman and social needs so lavishly?

Could you find anywhere in the Southwest a hostelry so perfect in all its appointments so amply equipped to serve you in the best manner and with so many of the luxuries of a semi-tropic country?

When **you** come to Galveston—for come you will, some day—be sure to **stop at Hotel Galvez—** where the best in the world awaits you.

RATES

Single room, per day	$ 2.50
Single room, by the week	15.00
Single room, with bath, per day	3.50 up
Single room, with bath, by the week	21.00 up

Rates for rooms en suite may be arranged for by correspondence. State full number in party and all special requirements.

HOTEL GALVEZ
P. E. SANDERS, MANAGER
GALVESTON, TEXAS
"The best in the world is Galveston at the Galvez"
GEO. S. KING, Manager

GOLF
Every Day in the Year

The Galveston Country Club has one of the finest 18-hole Golf Courses in the Southwest—designed by one of America's foremost Golf Architects. Guests of Hotel Galvez have all the privileges of this Course upon payment of a nominal Greens fee—15 minutes from the Hotel by automobile.

Bring your Golf Clubs and play upon a Course, immediately adjoining a portion of Galveston's famous Beach, fanned by the cool Gulf Breeze.

CLARKE & COURTS, GALVESTON

day during an interval between the third and final acts of the play *The Girl of the Golden West* to share the news with the audience of what had been accomplished. The news that the beachfront hotel was virtually guaranteed was greeted with enthusiastic and prolonged applause. When the applause died down, he invited everyone to remain after the performance for a few minutes for further information.

Following the final curtain call, John Henry Langbehn, who had pledged $11,000, and one of his associates shared details about the meeting at Cathedral Hall and the progress in fundraising. He then extended the opportunity for the audience to join the project by subscribing to the fund. A representative of the shipping agency Currie, Hawley & Company purchased three shares for $100 each on the spot.

When the story of the success of the initial subscriptions was printed in the local newspapers, others soon joined. Among those who subscribed $1,000 or more were John Henry Langbehn, Edwin Orville Flood, Maco Stewart, Albert Lasker, Morris Lasker, Mills Cornelius Bowden, Jockusch-Davidson & Company, Bishop Nicolaus Aloysius Gallagher (of the local Catholic diocese), Marx Marx Estate, Martin P. Morrissey, Henry Martyn Trueheart, Thomas Goggan & Sons, John Adriance & Sons, E.S. Levy & Company, William Turner Armstrong, Morris S. Ujffy, Robert Palliser, George Schneider & Company, William Parr & Company, John P. McDonough, Star Drug Store, Alfred S. Newson, the *Galveston Tribune* and Robert I. Cohen.

By the first week of March 1910, fundraising passed the half-million-dollar mark and a construction committee was appointed, consisting of Kempner, Sealy, Cooper, Armstrong, John Adriance, Charles Fowler, Peter G. Pauls, Stewart, Morris O. Nobbe and Edmund Reed Cheeseborough. This group elected a board of directors composed of Kempner (president), Adoue (first vice-president), Flood (second vice-president), Sealy (treasurer) and Langbehn (secretary).

Engraved certificates of stock were issued to the subscribers in April.

At their first official board meeting, the members decided to invite proposals from the most experienced hotel architectural firms from across the country, while the board focused on selecting a site for the hotel. After all proposals had been reviewed, six firms were invited to Galveston to present their plans before the board: Harvey, Page & Company of San Antonio; J. Flood Walker of San Antonio; Eames & Young of St. Louis; Warren & Welmore of New York; Banett, Hayucs & Barnett of St. Louis; and Mauran & Russell of St. Louis.

GALVESTON'S NEW BEACH HOTEL

HOTEL GALVEZ

FRONTING DIRECTLY ON BOULEVARD AND SEA WALL. 155 FT. LONG, 75 FT. WIDE. SIX STORIES AND BASEMENT. 250 ROOMS, ALL "OUTSIDE" AND OVERLOOKING GULF SUN PARLORS. CONVENTION ROOMS, ETC. PORCH AROUND ENTIRE FRONT, 750 FT. LONG, 18 FT. WIDE. STEEL REINFORCED CONCRETE CONSTRUCTION. ABSOLUTELY FIRE, WATER AND STORM PROOF. COST, FURNISHED, ONE MILLION DOLLARS.

Promotional concept drawing of Hotel Galvez, ca. 1911.

The vying design groups arrived on the island on April 6 and were divided into two groups: one that would present in the morning and one in the afternoon. The participating firms remarked that the vetting process devised by the board was one of the best methods they had encountered, ensuring that each firm had ample opportunity to review their materials with the deciding board.

At the end of a board meeting after the final presentation of the afternoon, Langbehn had the honor of announcing that the renderings of Ernest John Russell of Mauran & Russell had been chosen for the project.

Russell, a British-born architect, joined the firm in 1900 and had soon become a full partner. Considered one of the leading architects of the country, he played a role in the design of Houston's Rice Hotel and municipal auditorium, the Gunter Hotel in San Antonio, the Railway Exchange and Federal Reserve Bank buildings in St. Louis and many other prominent structures across the country.

Office space was arranged at the Texas Bank and Trust of Galveston to serve as a headquarters for Russell, where he could receive mail, telegrams and telephone calls.

In an effort to ensure the height of expertise for the assignment, the board also engaged Daniel Philip Ritchey of New York to work in conjunction with the architects. He was considered the foremost expert of his time in hotel planning and was known in the hospitality industry as the "Hotel Doctor."

Ritchey had a reputation for utilizing a scientific approach in planning hotel operations and arranging hotel interiors to function at the height of convenience for tourists and efficiency for staff.

The board decided on an ideal site for the structure at Twenty-First Street and Seawall Boulevard, and the officers of the Galveston Hotel Company quickly commenced purchasing lots from land, home and business owners situated there at the time. Most of the existing homes were small enough to be moved elsewhere on the island. Those whose land was purchased included the following: grocer Angelo Mangiapani, Caroline and Otto Ulrich, Martin P. Morrissey, Joseph L. Gengler, William H. Janssen, Mortiz Brock, James Boddeker, Joseph Louis Boddeker, John F. Moore of Houston, Maria Labarbera, Edward R. Girardeau, William H. Ott, Heinrich Muller, Frank and Catherine Ripper, John and Ellen Williams and a number of others. It was a daunting project, but the positive attitude the community had about the project made it possible.

On April 18, 1910, Mangiapani's Grocery Store, a two-story wood frame building, was the last hindrance to be removed from the new Galvez property. It was taken two blocks away to its new location at 2101 Avenue O$\frac{1}{2}$.

Russell and Ritchey arrived in Galveston the following day to present completed plans for a five-story structure. Speculation and excited rumors about the design rippled through the community, but Galvestonians were cautioned that the initial design would most likely evolve several times before construction began.

The full board was present, and the men spent the first meeting day reviewing and making changes to the design. Seeing the amount of work still to be accomplished, Russell telegraphed to St. Louis for two assistants, who arrived within two days. One of these men, William DeForrest Crowell, would become a partner with the firm before the Galvez project was completed.

Meetings were held for three days, with necessary adjustments incorporated in the designs each time. That Friday, Russell presented the revised designs to the board while Crowell and Ritchey visited the future construction site to make notes. While they were there, they were able to observe the derrick and rig that had been erected to drill a nine-hundred-foot artesian well to provide the hotel with an independent source of water.

The men departed that evening for St. Louis to make plans for a visit to the East Coast, where they would visit hotels that had already incorporated some of the features Ritchey suggested for the Hotel Galvez.

Bathhouse attractions on Seawall Boulevard between Twenty-Third and Twenty-Fourth Streets, circa 1907–14. *Author's collection.*

Immediately following their hotel tours, Russell and Ritchey sent minor design changes to the board that included shortening the two side wings and adding one more story to the center part of the structure. The team calculated that this adjustment would provide more room at less cost.

5

MEMBERS OF THE BOARD

A group of some of the most prominent and influential businessmen on the island served as the board of directors and officers of the Galveston Hotel Company, which organized the construction and held original ownership of the Hotel Galvez. Both before the construction of the hotel and in the years following, their efforts were directly responsible for the community's dream of a new beach hotel becoming a reality.

To list all of the business and personal accomplishments of these gentlemen would require a book in itself, but here is a brief introduction.

Hotel Galvez stationery, circa 1924. *Author's collection.*

Bertrand Adoue (1841–1911)

Born in Aurignac, France, Adoue came to the United States at the age of twenty.

The astute businessman was a partner of the Galveston firm Adoue & Lobit, which operated first as general merchandisers and later as bankers and cotton factors. He was also an active participant in the development of a number of industries and companies throughout the Southwest, holding positions that included being a director of A.H. Belo & Company (publisher of the *Galveston-Dallas News*), president of the Galveston Dry Goods Company, president of the Galveston Brewing Company, vice-president of the Lasker Real Estate Company, vice-president of the Galveston Hotel Company, treasurer of the Surf Bathing Company and president of the Osterman Widows and Orphans' Home Fund.

An important figure in the Société Français Beinfaisance of Galveston, he held the official position of consul for France, Norway and Sweden at the port of Galveston.

Adoue passed away just months after the grand opening of the Hotel Galvez. As a final act of generosity, he left $40,000 in his will for the Adoue Seaman's Bethel, providing bed, board, spiritual guidance and refuge to needy seafarers to this day.

Edmund Reed Cheesborough (1867–1961)

Texas native Cheesborough was a vital member of the Galveston Island community. In addition to being postmaster, secretary-treasurer of Texas Portland Cement and Lime Company, director and vice-president of South Texas State Bank, secretary-treasurer of the Galveston Terminal Company and secretary-treasurer of Leon and H. Blum Company, he also performed years of public service.

He served as secretary of the Galveston Cotton Carnival, was on the board of directors for the Young Men's Christian Association and was president of the board of the Galveston Commercial Association (which later merged with the Galveston Chamber of Commerce) for over three years.

His greatest contributions were made as secretary of the Grade Raising Board of the City of Galveston and member of the East End Flats Improvement Committee from 1903 to 1926. From orchestrating and managing the daunting task of having dredge material pumped from the bottom of the Gulf onto the island to achieve a grade raising, to handling unrest among citizens during the trying process, his impact was invaluable.

Harry Sidney Cooper (1854–1936)

Cooper came to Galveston in 1904 as general manager of the Electric Light & Street Railway Company, charged with the task of overseeing the reconstruction and reorganization of the railway during the grade-raising process.

When he finished that assignment for Stone & Webster Interests in 1910, he was retained to supervise the design and construction of the Hotel Galvez. After its completion, he moved to Dallas in 1913 to become executive secretary of the Southwestern Electric & Gas Association, the largest sectional organization of utility operators in the United States, and an engineering consultant for the construction, operation and management of electric lighting, electric railways and waterworks plants.

The British native and his wife returned to live in Galveston after retirement, remaining active in public affairs.

Edwin Orville Flood (1855–1938)

Flood moved from New York to Galveston as the father of a young family in the early 1880s.

A president of the Galveston Chamber of Commerce, Flood was active in Galveston civic affairs for many years.

He operated E.O. Flood & Company, a wholesale and retail coal business, in Galveston for thirty years and was associated with Texas's coal administration during the First World War. He also owned the steamship *Manteo*, which was used to transfer cargo from ships to barges, to facilitate easy transfer to the harbor.

Charles Fowler (1858–1931)

At the age of fourteen, Fowler, a native of Connecticut, went to sea. He became master of a vessel at twenty-one and remained a seaman until 1866, when he became the manager of the Morgan Lines shipping interests in Galveston.

Captain Fowler entered the naval branch of the Confederate service at the opening of the Civil War, taking an active part in the Battle of Sabine

Pass, after which he was taken prisoner. He was confined in prison at Fort Lafayette, New York, and Fort Warren, Boston, for about a year and a half, and then he was released. He returned to the Morgan Lines after the war, eventually taking charge of the Galveston offices.

Fowler was elected to the Galveston Board of Aldermen, was chairman of the city's finance commission and acted as an advisor to the financial community. He also was on the board of directors of Galveston Terminal Railway and held positions with eleven philanthropic associations in addition to his membership on the vestry of Trinity Episcopal Church.

Frank Jones (1843–1924)

Jones arrived in Galveston from Canada in 1869 and began work as a building contractor. Among the notable edifices for which he acted as contractor was the Clarke & Courts Building, which still exists today. His skills and advice were crucial in the planning stages of the Hotel Galvez.

He was president and one of the organizers of the Galveston Building & Loan Company, president of Peoples Loan & Homestead Company, vice-president of Real Estate and Loan Company and a trustee of Galveston

Souvenir photo taken by Russian photographer Louis Tobler in his studio at Murdoch's Bathhouse, circa 1935. *Author's collection.*

Public Schools. He also held offices with the Safety Deposit and Trust Company, Odd Fellows Building Association, Suburban Improvement Company and several other financial institutions.

He gave back to his island home by serving as a city alderman and a director on the boards of the Galveston Orphan's Home and the Letitia Rosenberg Women's Home.

Isaac "Ike" Herbert Kempner (1873–1967)

Kempner was a leading figure in Galveston finance, government, industry and philanthropy.

As the eldest son of Harris Kempner, Isaac took charge of the family's large cotton business at the age of twenty-one, when his father passed away. He and his brother Daniel expanded the business and branched out into real estate speculation.

After the 1900 Storm, he was named to the Galveston Relief Committee to restore living conditions. One of his most important legacies is being one of the originators of the commission form of city government after the disaster. He was the youngest man ever elected to the position of director for the Galveston Cotton Exchange in 1895 and later served in the capacity of president or vice-president for nearly fifty years.

Kempner and W.T. Eldridge acquired a twelve-thousand-acre sugar mill, plantation and refinery in Sugar Land in 1906, eventually expanding their control over the sugar-refining industry into a virtual monopoly by the 1930s. After Eldridge's death in 1932, the Kempner family consolidated this business under the name Imperial Sugar Company.

Governor Joseph Sayers appointed him a member of the Board of Commissioners of the City of Galveston. He became the city's first commissioner of finance and revenue, serving from 1901 to 1915 and serving as mayor from 1917 to 1919.

Director of the Gulf Colorado and Santa Fe Railway for more than fifty years, Kempner also acted as president and chairman of the board of the Texas Prudential Insurance Company and held a controlling interest in the United States National Bank in Galveston.

John Henry "Harry" Langbehn (1867–1945)

British native Langbehn immigrated to America in 1889 and immediately established himself as a dedicated, community-minded young man with a keen sense of business.

He worked for a time for J. Moller & Company Steamship Agents, and when the owner retired, Langbehn continued the business under the name Langbehn Brothers with his brother Frederick.

In addition to the steamship line responsibilities, he was chairman of the Central Committee for a Beach Hotel (the forerunner to the Galveston Beach Company), chairman of the Galveston Maritime Association, president of the Galveston Commercial Association, president of the Galveston Dry Dock & Company, director of American National Insurance Company, vice-commodore of the Galveston Boat and Yacht Club, president of Seaboard Lumber & Milling and president of the Galveston Business League. Langbehn was an officer with the News Publishing Company, Guaranty Federal Savings and Loan, Galveston Ice & Cold Storage Company, Stewart Title Company, Southern Beverage Company and Security National Fire Insurance Company.

He also served as honorary consul of Japan at Galveston. A representative of the Japanese government conferred the prestigious Order of the Rising Sun Fourth Class on Langbehn at a special reception at the Hotel Galvez in 1936, in recognition of his distinguished service.

John Hutchings Sealy (1870–1926)

A senior member of the banking house of Hutchings, Sealy & Company, cofounded by his father, Sealy was a member of the first graduating class of Ball High School in 1887.

Sealy was a leader during relief operations immediately following the 1900 Storm as well as in long-range planning and rebuilding, acting as chairman of the finance commission and proponent of the construction of the seawall and grade raising. In 1911, he bought several oil properties that he used to found the Magnolia Petroleum Company, which evolved into today's Mobil Oil.

He was vice-president and part owner of American Indemnity in addition to his holdings with the International Creosoting and Construction Company,

Galveston Ice & Storage Company, Texas Indemnity Company and Union Passenger Company. The banker was also elected president of both the Gulf, Colorado and Santa Fe Railway and the Galveston Wharf Company.

His philanthropic works included lifelong support of the John Sealy Hospital (named for his father) and serving on boards of the Letitia Rosenberg Home for Women and the Galveston Orphan's Home. He was also a trustee of the Galveston schools, founding board member and president of the Rosenberg Library and served as treasurer for the Diocese of Texas of the Episcopal Church.

Sealy was a brother-in-law of Robert Waverly Smith, another member of the Galveston Hotel Company.

Robert Waverly Smith (1865–1930)

An attorney, banker and civic leader, the Virginia-born Smith came to Galveston to practice law after graduating from the University of Texas.

President of the First National Bank of Galveston, he also held the office of city attorney for Galveston, was an active member of the Galveston Deep Water Project, was vice-president and director of the Galveston Wharf Company, was president of the Galveston Commercial Association, served on the board of directors of the Rosenberg Library Association and was part of the committee that formulated the commission form of government.

He and his wife, Jennie Sealy, established the Sealy Smith Foundation to provide health care in Galveston through the John Sealy Hospital, which was named for her father.

Maco Stewart (1871–1938)

Son of a Texas legislator, Maco Stewart I and his brother formed the Title Guarantee Company, offering the first title insurance in the state and later incorporated under the name Stewart Title Company. He served as president and attorney of the Galveston City Company, president of the Guaranty Federal Savings and Loan Association and attorney for the Standard Dredging Company.

Active in community affairs, Stewart was a member of the Rotary Club, director of Galveston Community Chest and president of the Galveston Provident Association, which was a united charities project.

Stewart, the largest landholder in the East End Flats of Galveston Island, donated six hundred acres of his own property adjacent to the Fort San Jacinto Military Reservation to the federal government for an eastward extension of the seawall.

6

BY ANY OTHER NAME

The new hotel remained nameless through the first few months of planning, which caused endless debates and discussions across the island as to what would be a proper choice.

Those who had fond memories of the hotel that formerly stood on the waterfront favored giving the new hotel the same name: the Galveston Beach Hotel. This was quickly dismissed by the Galveston Hotel Company's board of directors, who felt that the word *beach* suggested that the structure was directly on the beach itself and subject to danger from storms.

The hotel was planned to sit approximately six hundred feet in back of the new seawall and nineteen feet above beach level.

The original inn's name also gave the impression that it would only be a summer hotel and closed in the winter. This line of reasoning eliminated numerous other choices that had similar meanings, such as Beach Hotel, New Beach Hotel, Texas Beach Hotel, Gulf Beach Hotel, Gulf Front Hotel, Sea Breeze Hotel and Agua Vista (Spanish for "water view").

One unusual suggestion was Kempner on the Beach, as a tip of the hat to one of the community leaders who made the hotel possible, but Isaac Kempner himself was against the idea. Other proposals included the Colossus, referring to its grand size; the Comet, inspired by the highly publicized return of Halley's Comet in May 1910; the appropriately elegant name the Crystalline; El Mina, coincidently or not the name of the local Shriner's Temple founded in June 1902; San Jacinto, for a local historical

Hotel Galvez souvenir matchbook cover by Diamond Match company, undated. *Author's collection.*

battleground during the war for Texas's independence; and the Pelican, after an endearing native island waterfowl.

A popular choice was the Dixie, in hopes of luring people from across the nation to the warm southern beachfront. It was strongly recommended by New York hotel consultant D.P. Ritchey during his stay in Galveston and became by far one of the favorite options. After long deliberations, it was eliminated from the list by the board of directors because they felt the word had been cheapened in advertising campaigns for a variety of products and that it might have a negative connotation of being unwelcoming to visitors from northern cities.

In late June 1910, after construction had already begun, the directors made an official announcement of the name chosen for the new structure, putting any further debates to rest. After diligently reviewing all of the proposals, it was christened the Hotel Galvez by unanimous decision. The name and coat of arms of Bernardo de Gálvez with the motto "I alone" were deemed to be especially appropriate, as the people of Galveston alone, without outside funds, worked together to bring the hotel into existence.

7

BERNARDO DE GÁLVEZ

Hotel Galvez and Galveston Island were named in honor of Bernardo Vicente de Gálvez y Madrid, a daring Spanish officer who ironically never set foot in Galveston. Honored as an ally of Americans during the Revolutionary War, he is considered one of Spain's great military figures.

Born in the small village of Macharaviya in the province of Málaga, Spain, on July 23, 1746, he studied military science at the Academy of Ávila and began service in the Spanish military at age sixteen.

Thanks in part to his influential father and uncle, Gálvez ascended quickly in rank as he fought in the 1762 war against Portugal, against the Apache in Mexico in 1770 and in Spain's failed 1775 invasion of Algiers. He was dispatched to New Orleans in June 1777 and was appointed its interim governor of Spanish Louisiana at the age of thirty the following New Year's Day.

During the American Revolution, the Continental Congress sent a flotilla down the Ohio and Mississippi Rivers to New Orleans carrying a letter to Gálvez offering "hemp, flax, skins, furs, beef, [and] pork" to trade with Spain in exchange for military supplies and a loan of 150,000 gold coins. The young governor agreed, with the condition that word of his assistance would not be shared with England.

Shipments of gunpowder, muskets, fabric for uniforms, medicine and other supplies were sent to the American forces via the riverways, avoiding British blockades of the eastern ports. Spain, though officially neutral in the Revolutionary War, had a longtime rivalry with England, and assistance offered to the Continental army was strategically given in order to weaken the British forces.

In the summer of 1779, Spain officially declared war on England, and Gálvez gathered an army composed of his Spanish regulars, Creoles, free blacks and Native Americans to remove the British from Baton Rouge, Natchez and Mobile. This effectively forced the British to fight on two fronts simultaneously: against Spain in the south, and against the Continental army in the east.

Texas governor Domingo Cabello y Robles provided Gálvez with over ten thousand cattle for food and several hundred horses for his soldiers in what is considered the first Texas cattle drive from San Antonio to Louisiana.

After being delayed by a hurricane the previous fall, Gálvez attacked England's last remaining outpost at Pensacola, Florida, in the spring of 1781. A less daring Spanish naval commander who was part of the offensive hesitated to expose his fleet to British fire in the narrow Pensacola Harbor. Reportedly announcing "I alone" will go, Gálvez went forward on his ship *Galveztown* without him.

The battle continued for two months before the British soldiers surrendered and left Florida. The auxiliary benefit of this Spanish victory was that it removed the threat of British troops deploying from the south to fight against the Americans during the final battle at Yorktown, as well as allowing France to deploy its naval assistance to join in the decisive battles. George Washington and the U.S. Congress officially recognized Gálvez for his assistance during the American Revolution.

When Gálvez returned to Spain with his wife and children in the spring of 1783, Carlos III of Spain elevated him to the nobility as a reward for his victories over the British in West Florida during the Revolution. He gave Gálvez permission to use the phrase "Yo solo," which translates to "I alone," on his coat of arms, to commemorate his heroic actions at Pensacola.

The following year, he was called to serve as captain general and governor of Cuba, and in 1785, he succeeded his late father as viceroy of New Spain (now Mexico). Gálvez died of yellow fever in Mexico City on November 8, 1786, at the age of forty and was buried beside his father in the Church of San Fernando there.

In the 1820s, Mexico named Galveston, Texas, in tribute to the Spanish hero. As a part of the United States' bicentennial anniversary in 1976, a bronze equestrian statue of Gálvez was erected in Washington, D.C., to memorialize his service during the Revolution.

Color lithograph of Bernardo de Gálvez's family coat of arms.

On December 16, 2014, Gálvez was posthumously awarded honorary citizenship by the United States Congress and deemed a hero of the American Revolution. He was the first Spanish-speaking recipient of this honor, which has been bestowed on only seven other people, including Winston Churchill, Mother Teresa and the Marquis de Lafayette.

The Gálvez coat of arms, including the motto "Yo solo," was adopted by the city of Galveston and the Hotel Galvez as a symbol of resilience and self-sufficiency.

The original fine china of the hotel featured the crest surrounded with Galveston's signature oleander blossoms.

Taking a closer look at the symbols, or "charges," of a family crest reveals details about the person or family it was created to represent, and the Gálvez heraldry is no exception. The castle represents the capitol that he fought for, which was Madrid, and the rearing lion symbolizes courage, nobility and valor—vital characteristics for a good soldier.

Three round, gold circles depict coins, or "bezants," which are the emblem of someone worthy of trust and treasure. Two standing goats represent practical wisdom and victory. On the right side of the crest is the brigantine *Galveztown* with a portrayal of Gálvez on board holding a sword and the motto "Yo solo" flying overhead. In the center is a depiction of the small town where his family originated, with its famous oak tree and wolves that were native to the area. The fleur-de-lis was added as a symbol of Louisiana,

On the bottom of the shield are different symbols that indicate that Gálvez was awarded the title of nobleman for his military merit: a soldier's helmet, canons, flags, trumpets, drums, bow and arrow and even a tomahawk (war axe used by Native Americans).

Around the crest is a white-and-blue ribbon threaded through the Royal and Distinguished Order of King Carlos III medal, the highest military award in Spain.

More simplified versions of the elaborate crest were sometimes used.

Along with an array of other fancifully designed crests, the Gálvez coat of arms decorates the hotel lobby to this day.

8

CONSTRUCTING A QUEEN

The Hotel Galvez was built by one of the country's oldest contracting firms, James Stewart & Company. The St. Louis company's other accomplishments include St. Louis's Jefferson Memorial Building (now the Missouri History Museum), Detroit's Union Depot, the men's residential hall for Houston's Rice University and numerous courthouses across the nation.

Concrete-mixing equipment and other machinery for the construction arrived via the Southern Pacific Railway in late June. J.L. Jacobs, the construction superintendent, reached the island the previous day to receive the machinery and made preparations for its transportation to the work site.

While awaiting the arrival of more equipment, Jacobs and Harry Cooper, one of the board members, visited local contractors to arrange for preparatory work to begin. Because the Galvez was a distinctly Galveston undertaking, local labor was used whenever possible throughout the project.

Contracts for provision of wooden piles and pile driving took priority so work could begin within days. Others for sand, cement and gravel were next, with many of the materials arriving on site carried in two-mule carts.

One of the $1,000 subscribers, Mills C. Bowden, won the bid for lumber for his firm the Island City Woodworking Company. He had endeared himself to the community by building fifty-five two-room commissary houses in the months following the 1900 Storm to house survivors. He would later take part in the construction of the City Bank Building on Market Street and the Galveston Scottish Rite Temple. Galveston Gas

Fitting and Plumbing Company won the largest subcontracting project for installation of plumbing.

Pilings for the foundation were soon being driven into the ground. The thirty-foot-long trunks of full-grown trees were pushed into clay substrates of the property with a pile driver and a water jet until only the tops were visible, flush with the surface. To accomplish this, a gasoline engine pump was situated on the beach with a large hose that stretched over the seawall. Seawater was driven through the hose to a nozzle that applied over seventy pounds of pressure to each piling in turn, until its full length was driven into the ground. The water was then turned off and the pipe withdrawn from the hole, leaving the pile firmly in place. The water around the wood drained off through the soil.

A staggering 642 pilings were driven in groups of five and nine with about four feet of space between them, with sixty or seventy placed each day. Concrete piers were then erected on top of the groupings to form a foundation worthy of a fortress.

A rumor circulated around Galveston that the water obtained from the hotel's artesian well would be unfit to drink and suitable only for bathing or cooking. Board members extinguished these concerns by explaining that the well would be dug to a depth of eight hundred to nine hundred feet and went so far as to claim it would have medicinal value such as curing people of digestive problems. They also printed a chemical analysis of the water in the daily paper and proved that their well would be the same depth as was used by the local ice company, whose product was consumed across the island.

In July 1910, the Galveston Hotel Company requested permission from the city to lay two saltwater pipes through the seawall at the foot of Twenty-First Street across from the Hotel Galvez site to provide water for the hotel's pool. Though these pipes are long gone, it's still possible to view the point where they entered the wall from beach level.

The construction workers laid a corduroy road (a road made from tree trunks laid across a swampy area) from the street across the width of the property to facilitate the movement of heavy machinery, and erected storeroom sheds to hold supplies.

Concrete mixing machinery and steel rods to reinforce the walls were staged on-site, and a derrick erected to lift heavy loads of mixture into the molds was assembled. The massive "guy derrick" had support legs and a swinging boom arm attached to a central mast. Steel truss booms were also put into place in preparation of the first load of concrete.

Hotel Galvez construction site, 1910.

The slow progress of the ongoing grade raising of the island caused headaches during the construction of the Galvez. At one point, the crew had building material that included one hundred tons of structural steel lying on a lot staged for use. With only twenty-four hours' notice, the board was informed that the staging site would be needed for filling operations. They immediately stopped operations and redirected their entire workforce to move the steel and succeeded in transporting it to an alternate lot on Avenue P. The board also rushed to find a location to store a million bricks that were en route to the site. The filling operation given as a reason for the move, however, did not actually take place for over one week. Persevering, the crew drove the last of the numerous timbers into the site on August 15, and one month later, concrete for the floor of the basement was poured.

Galveston's enthusiasm for the progress of the construction of the grand hotel was visible in advertisements, newspaper stories and businesses. For a Galveston Day parade in August 1910, the E.S. Levy Department Store float featured a group of handsome young men modeling clothing from the store in front of a huge painting of the Hotel Galvez.

Structure for the ballroom of the Hotel Galvez presented unique challenges. The forty-by-sixty-foot room was designed to create a sweeping, open space for dancing with no columns to interrupt its flow. This required heavy beams and girders reinforced with steel as support beneath the dance floor and for the wings above it. The few columns that did exist in the plans were heavily reinforced as well. Wooden forms for the concrete columns of the second floor were completed in October and the concrete poured for the columns and slabs.

In late October, a group of Japanese businessmen including Baron Mitsui visited the island for meetings regarding a planned Yokohama-Galveston steamship service scheduled to begin in time for the opening of the new Panama Canal. Their grand tour of the city included the seawall and impressive construction site of the new hotel. Though it appeared as a great mass of concrete and steel rods, the businessmen showed genuine appreciation of the engineering feat and were said to have taken numerous photographs.

View of beachgoers from a pier in front of Hotel Galvez, showing trolley car, circa 1911.

Within weeks, the concrete of the second-story floor hardened and preparations began to construct the third floor in November. Wooden forms around the set concrete of the basement level were removed except for the area beneath the ballroom, where they were left in place longer as a precautionary measure due to the weight they would bear.

The third floor was complete by the end of the month, and work on the fourth floor began in December. This cyclical work continued until each story of the hotel had been completed.

The construction site was often lined with spectators, and the workers jokingly dubbed the bystanders as members of the Order of the Sons of Rest, being happy to watch others do the work.

Galveston Electric Company began rebuilding the track and trolley pole line along Seawall Boulevard between Twenty-First and Twenty-Second Streets in mid-May 1911. This process provided the opportunity to eliminate half of the poles previously used by situating the poles in the center of the boulevard rather than all to one side. The tangle of necessary wires was also relocated to Avenue Q, allowing a less obstructed view of the Gulf from atop the seawall.

When this work was completed, Twenty-First Street from Avenue P to the Seawall and all streets surrounding the new hotel were paved with brick to replace the mud shell roads.

9

AN EXPERT STAFF

The directors of the Galveston Hotel Company selected John Franklin "Jack" Letton to manage the new hotel. Formerly manager of the Hotel Bentley in Alexandria, Louisiana, Letton signed a ten-year management contract for the Hotel Galvez.

He insisted on choosing a staff with impeccable skills and recruited his workforce of managers, stewards, waiters and clerks from such elite hotels as the Grand Hotel at Mackinac, London's Ritz-Carlton, New York's Hotel Knickerbocker, Charleston's Hotel Ruffner, Cleveland's Euclid and the Blackstone in Chicago.

By the end of May 1911, almost the entire workforce of the Hotel Galvez had arrived in Galveston. Among the first staffers Letton hired was Charles B. Nagel, superintendent of service, who came to the Galvez from the Hotel Rector in New York City. He had previously worked at the Ritz-Carlton Company of London and Paris for fourteen years, as well as New York's Hotel Astor and Hotel Knickerbocker.

Nagel brought three of his headwaiters from New York's Hotel Rector to Galveston as well: Richard Newman Jr. had also worked for the Hotel Belmont; Harry Pacyna had previously served at the Hotel Plaza and Hotel Belmont in New York City; and C.T. Ambrose was formerly at the Ritz-Carlton in London and New York's Hotel Knickerbocker.

The steamship *Brazos* of the Mallory Line pulled into the harbor on Saturday, May 27, bringing the additional thirty-one waiters hired by Nagel in New York to provide table service at the Galvez. They were the last of the staff to arrive.

Twenty-First Street entrance and hotel manager John "Jack" Letton, 1911.

Letton had prearranged housing for his workers. The hotel manager (Letton himself), assistant manager, superintendent of service, head of housekeeping, steward and those holding a few other key positions would reside in the staff quarters at the hotel. Other positions were so numerous that additional accommodations were required.

Letton leased the nearby hotel known as Ocean House on the southeast corner of Avenue Q and Twenty-Fifth Street to provide initial housing for the first two years, having renovated the entire complex before his staff's arrival. It served as the permanent home of the cooks and waiters of the Galvez. Letton's wife, Mattie Elizabeth, lived there as well and served as a proprietress and "dorm mother" for the employees. The new residents were so charmed by Mrs. Letton that they refused to call the hotel Ocean House, preferring Villa Elizabeth instead.

Virtually every person employed at the hotel with the exception of William H. Driver, a former Galveston police officer hired as a watchman, was brought in from out of state.

Head steward Samuel Lachland came from New York City. Before working on the East Coast, he was associated with the Planters Hotel in St. Louis, the Grand Hotel at Mackinac and two famous San Francisco cafés: Tait's and Zinkand's. Assistant manager T.C. Metoyer formerly held the same position at New Orleans's St. Charles Hotel. Letton found his ideal chef, Fernand Montlouis, at New York's Waldorf Astoria. Head of housekeeping Mary E. Palmer came to Galveston from Hotel Ruffner in Charleston, West Virginia. Before that, she was employed at the Euclid in Cleveland, Ohio.

J.S. Brodorick, the night clerk, was also hired from the Ruffner and had previously worked at the Hotel Windsor in Wheeling, West Virginia. The chief bookkeeper and cashier, C.W. Moors, came to the Galvez from the Blackstone Hotel in Chicago, Illinois.

Charles W. Lennobacker, room clerk, was formerly of the Hotel St. Claire in Detroit, Michigan, and the fabulous Park Hotel of Hot Springs, Arkansas. Another room clerk, J. Herbert Stafford, had worked at both the Patten in Chattanooga, Tennessee, and the Gayoso in Memphis.

J. Vernon Fox, a front office cashier, had worked at the Hotel Ottawa in Ottawa Beach, Michigan, as well as various Denver hotels. Joseph Vickermann, also a front office cashier, was hired from the Hotel Biscayne of Miami, Florida.

Hotel Galvez dining room, 1911.

The manager of the buffet and bar, Frank Fuller, was appropriately hired from the elegant Seelbach Hotel in Louisville, Kentucky, which was known for its lavish special events.

These employees brought with them skill sets learned at the finest hotels across the nation, ready to help create memorable visits for the guests of the Hotel Galvez.

As with any large staff, some drama and changes ensued after the initial opening. In early July, seventeen waiters left the service of the hotel as a group. Management reported that they were discharged due to unsatisfactory service, while the men maintained that they left at their own decision. A group of seventeen replacements was immediately hired from New Orleans.

10

GRAND OPENING

Due to the anticipation and excitement surrounding the new beachfront beauty, Hotel Galvez had two opening events a month apart from each other.

The Galveston Chamber of Commerce and owners of the Hotel Galvez launched a wide-ranging advertising campaign to announce the imminent opening of their grand hotel on the seawall. An immediate response was received in the form of letters, telegrams and phone calls requesting reservations at the first opportunity.

The enthusiasm about the hotel resulted in management's decision to open the doors of the Galvez to guests on June 10, before the final details of decor were in place.

Hotel Galvez had already hosted special events, including a banquet and reception at 7:00 p.m. on June 8 for Rear Admiral Aaron Ward, the second in command of the Atlantic Fleet; General Albert L. Mills, Medal of Honor recipient; Captain William F. Fullam of the USS *Mississippi*; and other ranking officers of the army and navy who arrived in the port of Galveston that week. The gathering consisted of one hundred people—fifty hosts and fifty guests—and was hosted by the City of Galveston. Ward, Mills and Fullam had the honor of being the first to sign the Hotel Galvez guest register the previous day.

Hotel Galvez officially opened its doors to overnight guests on Saturday, June 10, 1911, at 6:00 p.m. and was immediately dubbed the "Queen of the Gulf," an endearing title it still holds.

Panoramic view of the Hotel Galvez loggia facing east, circa 1911.

Countless conventions have been held at Hotel Galvez over the years, including this one of the Phi Chi International Medical Fraternity in 1916. *Author's collection.*

George M. Dealy of Dallas made the first recorded reservation. The guest rate for single rooms was $2.00 per night, or $12.00 per week. Rates for rooms with private baths, quite a luxury, were slightly more expensive at $2.50 per night for singles and $16.00 per week.

The first of countless groups to hold an annual convention at the Galvez was the Texas Cotton Seed Crushers Association in late June 1911. A meeting of the Texas General Passenger Association took place at the hotel on June 14 to discuss and set railroad passenger rates for the coming season, which would directly affect future visitors to the Galvez.

Interurban car and automobiles crossing causeway, circa 1912.

Final details in decor and furnishings were finally in place the next month, and the Hotel Galvez was ready to take its place in hotel history in style.

In a special grand opening preview event on Monday, July 10, Texas newspapermen were guests at a banquet in the Automobile Room. Hotel manager Letton occupied the head of the table beside L.C. Bradley, manager of the Galveston-Houston Interurban and Galveston Railways.

The eye-catching centerpiece was a vine of electrically illuminated red and white roses accented with natural red and white carnations that wound across a spotless, white linen tablecloth. Hand-painted menu cards, each with a distinct cover illustration, served as unique souvenirs of the occasion.

At 8:00 p.m., superintendent of service Charles B. Nagle and hotel chef Fernand Montlouis provided attendees with an elaborate dinner, presented in a smoothly flowing system of service. The menu included Canape National (hors d'oeuvres), Crème de Volaille (cream of chicken soup), olives, almonds, Pompano Maître d'Hôtel (broiled fish with sauce), Médallon de Filet-de Boeuf (beef medallion), jardiniere (mixed vegetables), Bouchée de vol-au-vent Toulouse (puffed pastry appetizer), Punch Romaine, pigeons farcis plemontaise (stuffed pigeons with parmaesan and butter), Salade Galvez, Bronx cocktail, Zeltinger (Reisling), Pommery Sec (champagne), Grand Liquere and Apollnaris (German sparkling water).

Satisfied diners enjoyed after-dinner cigars as they listened to impromptu toasts and speeches by their host and fellow guests, proclaiming the beauty of the new hotel.

If you're ready to experience a bit of that landmark night for yourself, here are recipes for two of the cocktails served:

Bronx cocktail

2 ounces gin
¼ ounce dry vermouth
¼ ounce sweet vermouth
1 ounce fresh orange juice
A dash of orange bitters

In a shaker filled with ice, shake and strain into a chilled glass and serve.

Punch Romaine

Punch Romaine is a froth drink that was also served to first-class passengers of the Titanic after their final dinner aboard the following year.

1 egg white
1 ounce white rum
½ ounce simple syrup
½ ounce fresh lemon juice
1 ounce fresh orange juice
Champagne
Orange peel

Combine egg white, rum, simple syrup, lemon juice and orange juice in a cocktail shaker. Shake without ice, then add ice to the shaker and shake again until chilled. Strain into a snifter filled with crushed ice and top with champagne. Garnish with orange peel.

A much-anticipated grand opening of the Hotel Galvez took place on Wednesday afternoon, July 12, 1911. Though the hotel and restaurants had been open to customers for the previous month, the final details of the magnificent structure were finally in place.

The community was invited to an open house from 3:00 to 6:00 p.m. to enjoy a reception and a full tour of Galveston's newest source of pride. An astounding crowd of five thousand Galvestonians arrived at the celebration, traveling by automobiles, carriages, streetcars and on foot.

Left: Hotel Galvez information pamphlet, 1911.

Below: Hotel Galvez ballroom arranged for day lounging, circa 1925. *Author's collection.*

Opening day of the Hotel Galvez, June 1910.

The lobby was festively decorated, and visitors enjoyed punch while listening to selections played by the Hotel Galvez Orchestra throughout the afternoon. Many made immediate plans to return on learning that, after opening day, the house orchestra would furnish music each day during lunch, afternoon tea and dinner, and in the ballroom or parlors in the evening.

Letton greeted the guests as they arrived, and his entire staff was on hand to ensure that visitors would enjoy themselves. Attendants were stationed throughout the hotel to answer questions and explain special features of the building as guests wandered through the cafés, kitchen, corridors and special suites that were open for inspection.

Directors and stockholders of the Galveston Hotel Company also proudly attended the festivities, delighting in the reaction of the community.

By the end of the day, the hotel had guest bookings for winter from New York, St. Louis, Kansas City, St. Joseph and numerous other northern cities.

Letton received dozens of congratulatory telegrams from Los Angeles to New York, and within a year, *Hotel Monthly* proclaimed the Hotel Galvez the "best arranged and most richly furnished seaside hotel in America."

11

QUEEN OF THE GULF

By the time the Hotel Galvez opened in 1911, every effort had been made to incorporate the finest details and amenities for guests. The commanding appearance of the Spanish Colonial Revival building, with an eight-story center section and two six-story wings, along with its gracious interiors, soon earned it the nickname "Queen of the Gulf."

Advertisements for the hotel included declarations that it was a fireproof structure, to allay any concerns that remained from the loss of the Beach Hotel.

The concrete structure was covered with brick and featured applied stucco finish. Crushed red Texas granite was mixed into the stucco to achieve a warm pinkish tone that almost seemed to glow in the sunsets. Its Spanish red-tile roof with large overhang supported by heavy wood cornices provided a distinctive appearance among other structures along the seawall.

The three entrances, facing north, south and west, each featured a marble plaque with the hotel name and a unique embellishment. The two wings projected from the center section toward the sea created the Palm Court that was landscaped with palms and Galveston's signature oleanders.

The central section of the hotel contained the majority of the rooms, and the corners of its central tower were adorned with four copper-roofed hexagonal towers. The topmost windows were trimmed with pilasters and featured arched windows, echoing those on the first floor. A separate four-sided tower jutted above the roofline near the southeast corner of the central section.

Come to Galveston
Via Any of These Railroads or Steamship Lines

M. K. & T.
Frisco
Santa Fe
Southern Pacific
Trinity & Brazos Valley
Galveston, Houston & Henderson
Houston & Texas Central
Missouri Pacific
St. Louis, Iron Mountain & Southern
International & Great Northern
Colorado & Southern
Cotton Belt Route
Rock Island Lines
Texas Midland
Ft. Worth & Denver City Ry.
Texas Central R. R.
Atchison, Topeka & Santa Fe
Kansas City Southern Ry.
Southern Ry.
Illinois Central R. R.
Chicago & Eastern Illinois
Chicago & Alton
Burlington Route
San Antonio & Aransas Pass
New Orleans & Pacific
Mallory Line
Atlantic Fruit & Steamship Co.

But

Come to Galveston

A Section of Central Park

WHEN you come to Galveston —as everybody does some day, lured by the best climate, the best surf bathing, the best hunting and fishing anywhere in the world—you will find also one of the very best, most commodious and luxurious hotels in the world —The GALVEZ!

You will miss no detail of service at Hotel Galvez. This magnificent hostelry is the tangible expression of Galveston's belief that she has the best in the world to offer the traveler, the sightseer, the sportsman, the pleasure seeker. The hotel was erected by public subscription for more than one million dollars, in order that every stranger within the gates might enjoy to the full this "little Cosmopolis of the Gulf Coast."

Nowhere is there another Galveston! The island city is unique—an objective for every world tourist. It is known far and wide as the sportsman's paradise, home of the monster Tarpon and other game denizens of the deep—Red Snapper, Spanish Mackerel, etc. Where can you find such hunting, such fishing, sailing, or better motoring, finer golf or such exhilarating surf bathing?

Bustling wharves outline the bay-side of the City of Galveston, where, in the finest harbor in the world,

Left and next two pages: Hotel Galvez brochure, circa 1920.

The Sun Parlor

A Corner of the Ball Room

merchant ships from every clime exchange heavy cargoes with Galveston. Hers is a world-part in trade, for the Port of Galveston is second only to New York.

Government battleships and army transports ride at anchor off Fort Crockett on the mainland, and army life is a feature of Galveston's social gayety.

Proud as Galveston is of her mammoth wharves, spread with acres of cotton bales and cargoes of every description, it is a lighter, more buoyant side the city turns toward the visitor. The pride of her citizens is shown in the beauty of her well-kept streets and handsome residences. Not only unparalleled beauties of Nature adorn Galveston lavishly, but some of the greatest construction and engineering marvels of the age are to be found at Galveston—the Causeway, the $15,000,000 Jetties, the tried and tested Sea Wall, and the famous experi-

ment in Grade Raising—now no longer an experiment.

Summer and winter—all seasons are delightful at Galveston.

The sun shines more than 300 days in every year. Winter travelers seek us for our place in the sun and return again in summer to share our Gulf breezes. The climate is ideally equable, with an average winter temperature of 65 170 degrees from October to June.

Along the Gulf side of the city —the play-side—stretches the famous Sea Wall—an impregnable bulwark against tempests and tides— 17 feet high, measuring 16 feet at the base and 5 feet at the top. Below it stretches the smooth, hard beach —extending either side far beyond the limits of Galveston for 30 miles. There is nothing else like this in all the world.

Hotel Galvez stands in a plaza of palms and oleanders, fronting the Sea Wall and looking out over the Gulf.

Hotel Galvez overlooks the 40-mile beach of Galveston—the finest in the World

"Open Season"

"Fisherman's Luck"

Named for the old Spanish Governor of the territory back in the 18th Century, Hotel Galvez is in that best type of Spanish Mission architecture which lends itself so perfectly to modern spacious hotel requirements. It is built of solid concrete and fireproof, of course. Rising six stories high it accommodates 500 guests and affords every comfort and convenience.

Entering the Lobby the visitor feels at once the standards of Hotel Galvez in the perfection and completeness of all furnishings. Nothing is left to accident. The most jealous regard for details makes a decorative ensemble which gives Hotel Galvez the distinctive atmosphere of an exclusive club or private home of wealth. Truly you find the "best in the world" at Hotel Galvez.

While the climate is "all outdoors" the comforts and attractions of indoors at Hotel Galvez inveigle many an hour from the visitor. Music of the highest

class is rendered by the Hotel Galvez Orchestra, with delightful programs daily in the loggia and again in the lounging room in the evening, while an orchestra is supplied during dinner. The finest social life in the city centers around Hotel Galvez and its Grand Ball Room lends brilliancy and gayety to every season. Galveston is a city of traditions, with passionate regard for the old ideals. Her people love to surround social intercourse with the charm and grace of the old regime.

Many distinguished names appear on the hotel register. Men of affairs find the environment of Hotel Galvez ideal for complete relaxation. At any season it offers the perfection of comfort, with rest and recreation, without cutting vital business ties. Two direct steamer lines to New York and the most complete railway connections for all parts of the country make it easy to get in and out of Galveston.

Scenes About Galveston

What true lover of line and gun can overlook the teeming waters, the populous nooks and bayous and prairies which surround Galveston? Here the migratory water fowl abound from early Fall till Spring. Quail and rabbit seem inexhaustible and hundreds of gamy fish are but a few hours' sport with reel or squid. Come to Galveston and match your skill with our Speckled Trout, or mighty Tarpon from the deep. Come and taste Canvasback, Mallard, Teal and Redhead at their best. Needless to say the Hotel Galvez offers the best of game, with sea-foods in finest perfection, including native crabs and oysters—the best in the world at Galveston.

Bathing, boating, tennis, golfing—every outdoor longing is answered by a sojourn on Galveston Island. A great deal of pleasure can be crowded into a week-end, but there is variety enough to make a long season one of endless delight for every visitor here. On the mainland, the Oleander Country Club, just 12 miles from Galveston, offers many additional benefits, including one of the finest golf courses to be found in this country, which guests of Hotel Galvez may arrange to share if they desire.

But the sport of sports is sea-bathing, in the invigorating waters of the Gulf of Mexico, on the hard,

smooth beach which has made Galveston famous. Here is admittedly the finest surf-bathing to be found anywhere in the world. There is no treacherous undertow, but the gentle sloping beach insures security. Here the invalid gathers health and strength and long hours are swiftly sped watching the gay crowds on the beach and the frolics of the breakers. Thanks to the warming Gulf Stream there is always good bathing at Galveston and the season is at its height, of course, from the end of March to November.

Could you find anywhere in the world a spot more delightful for your Winter or Summer play-ground—or one answering your sportsman and social needs so lavishly?

Could you find anywhere in the entire Southwest a hostelry so perfect in all its appointments, so amply equipped to serve you in the best manner and with so many of the luxuries of a semi-tropic country?

When *you* come to Galveston—for come you will, some day—be sure to *stop at Hotel Galvez*—where the best in the world awaits you.

RATES

Single room, per day - - - - -	$ 2.00
Single room, by the week - - - -	12.00
Single room, with bath, per day -	2.50
Single room, with bath, by the week,	16.00

Rates for rooms en suite may be arranged by correspondence. State full number in party and all special requirements. Address personally

P. L. SANDERS, Acting Manager

HOTEL GALVEZ

Galveston, Texas

"The best in the world in Galveston at the Galvez"

Hotel Galvez original entrance porte cochere, circa 1915.

The original front entrance to the hotel faced north to Avenue P (now known as Bernardo de Galvez Avenue), away from the Gulf, and is what many people consider the back entrance today. The porte cochere provided a grand entrance for the arrival of the vehicles of the day and features the hotel's name and Galvez coat of arms. The current staff fondly refers to it as the "locals entrance," since many BOIs (born on the island) and longtime residents prefer its informality.

Bavarian-born Paul Martin Heerwagen, one of the most widely respected interior decorators of the era, decorated the hotel. His other work included the Hotel Piedmont in Atlanta; Hotel Gay Teague in Montgomery, Alabama; the Peabody Hotel in Memphis; the Adolphus Hotel in Dallas; and the Arkansas State Capitol in Little Rock. An expert in the ornamentation of wall surfaces, his design offered a scheme that easily flowed from one area to the next.

Woodwork throughout the hotel was largely mahogany and Circassion walnut, a light brown wood from Russia distinguished by irregular black veins. In the lobby, square marble columns were ornamented with detailed, bronze acanthus leaf capitals that supported dark, mahogany beams overhead.

A nearby staircase to the lower level was crafted of white Carrerra marble and had a wrought-iron railing that is still visible on the left side.

Visitors could relax in the elegant walnut furniture upholstered in Spanish leather as they waited for other members of their party to descend to the

Main lobby of Hotel Galvez, with reception counter at the back, 1911.

lobby in the two cage-style electric passenger elevators or stroll across the terrazzo floor to deposit a Hotel Galvez postcard in the bronze mail shoot.

A painting of Count Bernardo de Gálvez, a copy of the original portrait in the National Art Gallery of Mexico City, hung at the western end of the promenade and was greatly admired by guests.

Modeled after a luxury hotel on the east coast of Florida, the Hotel Galvez had its own jewelry store in a room near the lobby. The Galveston firm of M.O. Nobbe & Company, the same firm that supplied silverware for the Galvez, spent over $2,000 fitting out the space, which offered a line of gold and silver articles and gems, in addition to a collection of high-class novelties in precious metals.

On opening day, the bar of the hotel featured dramatic black-oak paneled walls and a hand-carved black-oak bar. Though the bar that visitors see today is different, it has quite a history of its own. Originally a fixture in the first Tremont Hotel downtown in 1876, it was later moved to the Old Galveston Club, Galveston's last speakeasy. Happy customers imbibed spirited beverages around this counter throughout Prohibition. Local lore (though many swear it's fact) tells that Santos Cruz, the bartender who served over this same bar, also invented the margarita as a special drink for singer Peggy Lee, whose full first name was Margaret.

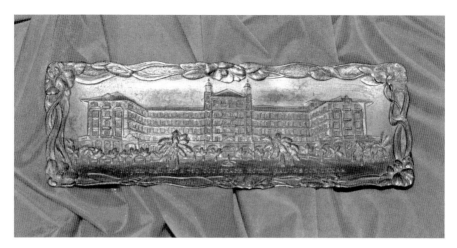

Sterling silver souvenir pin tray with relief of Hotel Galvez.

When the Old Galveston Club closed in 1992, George Mitchell purchased the beautiful bar and had it refurbished and installed at the Hotel Galvez.

The 1911 Marine Restaurant, where guests could enjoy club breakfasts and table d'hôte dinners, was separated from the east loggia by a series of windows set into archways that echoed the windows facing the Gulf.

When a new grill opened in 1919 operating much like today's self-serve buffets, the concept was so new to Galvestonians that instructions on how to use it ("First take a tray, knife, fork and spoon…") were published in the newspaper.

A few of the Marine's original features are still visible in the Galvez Bar and Grill today, including the cove ceilings, dental moldings and column capitals embellished with cherubs, laurel leaves, seashells and a *G* monogram.

During the tours at the hotel's grand opening, the east wing kitchen with its cutting-edge, labor-saving devices was met with enthusiastic interest from the public and press. It was regarded to be the most completely equipped American hotel of its time. Hotel manager Letton designed the one-hundred-by-fifty-foot kitchen himself to incorporate the finest equipment and create an expedient flow of service traffic.

A bakery occupied one corner of the room, next to a fully equipped butcher shop featuring a "silent" meat chopper. The variety of state-of-the-art equipment from John Van Range Company of Cincinnati was so extensive that the company mentioned the Galvez in its advertisements.

A seemingly endless line of ranges, ovens and grills stretched across the room, with gleaming copper soup cauldrons, pots and pans standing by ready

Windows of the Marine Dining Room opened to capture coastal breezes in the days before air conditioning.

for use. Among the revolutionary conveniences was an electric potato peeler that could process one bushel of potatoes in fifty seconds. Several varieties of vegetables could be cooked at the same time in the separated compartments of a special steam chest, and a separate steam table kept roasts at an even serving temperature.

Reviewers were equally impressed that the series of iceboxes contained no actual ice, being cooled by refrigeration through pipes. These lined the walls, with separate refrigerators for fish and poultry, oysters, wild game, milk, ice cream, ice, beer and wine each maintaining the ideal temperature for its contents. The hotel's ice cream was created in the first electric motorized ice-cream maker in the state of Texas.

Other fascinating inventions available to the kitchen staff were an electric butter pat cutter, bread crumbers, knife cleaners, an ice chopper, roll warmers and a series of egg boilers. A large and complex apparatus washed dishes and kept them heated in special compartments, ready for service.

Letton knew that it would require more than equipment to run the finest hotel kitchen and designed a system of service that ensured waitstaff would never have to retrace their steps in the process of serving guests. Entering from a service corridor, the waiter would travel in one direction in a circular path to avoid confusion or getting in another server's way. An underground corridor was provided for waiters to take food from the kitchen in the east end to the banquet hall in the west to avoid adding any traffic or noise in the guest spaces above. The plated food was conveyed in compartments of wheeled steam tables that kept the items at the proper temperature until it was time to serve them.

Steward supplies were kept in a thirty-two-foot-long chest near the service corridor. Staff used a separate back staircase to access a large banquet hall on the sixth floor.

Representatives from hotels around the country came to the Hotel Galvez in the months following its opening to learn from the highly organized system.

Daily menus and special hotel newspapers were printed in the basement's printing press room. The motor-driven press was also used to create customized place cards and printed mementos for special occasions at the hotel.

Directly below the bar, on the basement level, was a concrete cave wine room with wooden wine bins and its own cooling system. This room also housed a carbonator and a Blakeslee cube cutter used to saw ice into various sizes required by the bar and kitchen.

A barbershop, where the famous Galvestonian Sam Maceo once worked, was in the west end of the basement, as well as valet and tailor services, a doctor's office and a drugstore with a soda fountain and a candy shop. The inviting Galvez Spa where guests now visit stands where the barbershop and doctor's office were located in 1911.

The soda fountain, the most elaborate of its kind in Galveston, was a favorite of locals as well as visitors and had its own entrance on Avenue P. When it was first announced that the ice cream was made with electric machines instead of by hand, a group of indignant local women came to test it for themselves. The product earned their approval.

A tempting candy counter offered sweets created by the famous Repetti's Candy Company in New York. Charles Repetti, a master confectionary artist from Genoa, Italy, earned a gold medal at the Milan Exposition for his Swiss and Italian chocolates, caramels, glace nuts and candy pebbles. His peanut brittle was a Galvez favorite.

Spacious twin loggias, or promenades, adjoined the lobby spanning across the south side of the Galvez with large arched windows that could be opened so summer breezes filtered through fine mesh bronze screens, providing a refreshing space for guests to linger. Both loggias were decorated with laurel

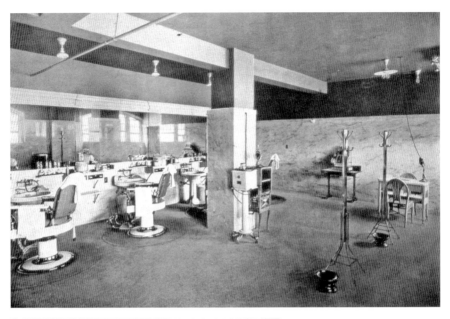

Above: Hotel barber shop, 1911.

Left: 1911 newspaper advertisement for Hotel Galvez ice cream and soda fountain.

THE ICE CREAM AND SODA FOUNTAIN ROOM OF HOTEL GALVEZ

IS NOW OPEN. THE FINEST IN THE CITY.

A fine line of the Famous REPITTI CANDIES is to be found here

When you go to the Beach visit this up-to-date establishment.

leaf stenciling along the ceiling, which has recently been refurbished. Also known as the Sun Parlor, it was furnished with white wicker chairs, sofas and tables, much as it appears today. It was an ideal location to enjoy the Gulf view and to people-watch.

The latter pastime led to the nickname "Peacock Alley" for the west loggia, where guests and visitors came to see and be seen in finery so grand it was said to "shame the proudest peacock." Originally twenty-five feet wide, part of the original Peacock Alley has been absorbed by the adjoining meeting rooms, which were once smaller parlors known as the Reading Room and Writing Room.

Just beyond the parlors was the Music Hall, designed to be used for events with bands and other performers. Musicians sat in a balcony between the two doorways. The elegant ivory-colored room with accents of gold was

Hotel soda fountain and drugstore, 1911.

The famous Peacock Alley at Hotel Galvez, 1911.

Writing Room off west loggia and Peacock Alley, 1911.

at one time called the Grecian Room, due to the watchful gaze of Greek goddesses above the doorways.

The east loggia leading to the terrace and veranda is now referred to as the "new" Peacock Alley.

At the north end of the east wing was a clubroom and bar specifically designed for gentlemen guests. Paneled in dark oak and furnished in Spanish Renaissance style, it featured a mezzanine-level grill with nooks for private conversation where men could broker deals, play chess or enjoy a cigar and brandy with their cronies. It is said that if wives went to search for their husbands in this area, they were denied admittance, and male guests soon learned it was a safe refuge from spouses and families.

Visitors today can see what remains of railing spindles of the level that once overlooked the massive bar level by standing outside of the Galvez gift shop and looking up.

The space now named the Terrace Dining Room was once the site of some of the most lavish events attended on the island. Featuring a round bay of windows overlooking the Gulf, it mirrored the Music Hall of the west wing from the exterior. Construction of the ballroom was one of the most daunting challenges in the construction of the Galvez, because designers wished to minimize the use of columns to maximize the floor space for dancing. Those few columns that were constructed are topped with acanthus leaves and mythical Pegasus figures at the corners.

The veranda surrounds the terrace and was originally a curved open-air space where guests could visit and enjoy views of the Gulf, gardens and pool.

When the hotel first opened, a pool existed in roughly the same position that one does today. Galvez guests were privy to this private luxury, filled with seawater from the Gulf, and used it rather than visiting the public bathhouses across the street.

In the extreme east end of the hotel were four private dining rooms, each decorated with a special theme. Light fixtures in the Modern Navigation room were in the shape of ships' steering wheels suspended by marine cables. Electric lights replaced the protruding spokes where a steerman's hands would grasp the outer rim of the wheels, and a ship's lantern hung beneath each wheel to provide additional lighting and atmosphere.

The Automobile Room, especially popular with the gentlemen, was illuminated with heavy brass automobile lanterns, and oil paintings of automobile races graced the walls. Likewise, the garden-like decor of the Arbor Room and the details of the Ancient Navigation Room also reflected their names.

The original design of the hotel provided for 275 guest rooms, 225 of which had private baths. Even the most basic room offered a single bed, vanity, chest, mirror, chair, electric lamps and chandeliers, telephone, steam heat and a sink with hot and cold running water. Writing desks were supplied with stationery and pens.

Nearly all the bedroom furniture was manufactured in Grand Rapids, Michigan, by William A. Berkey Furniture and the Oriel Cabinet Company. French prints adorned the walls, the windows were draped with English scrim curtains and Holland (fabric roller) shades and the doorknobs were made of glass. Walls that were not decorated were finished in a shade of navy gray believed to create a cool, resting effect.

No less attention was given to the appearance of the hallways, whose hard-oiled, glossy walls were trimmed with curved baseboards. Hall floors were covered with patterned Bundhar weave carpeting by Wilton, the same type made especially for the Fairmont Hotel in San Francisco.

A central vacuum system was installed throughout the hotel to maximize the efficiency and pace of the housekeeping staff.

From the beginning, the Hotel Galvez has been a favored choice of wedding parties, and in 1911, the public had its first glimpse of three bridal suites. All three were situated in the west wing overlooking the seawall and a long expanse of beach.

The second-floor bridal suite's light green walls provided a gentle backdrop for the Louis XVI furnishings finished in gold and ivory. The blue third-floor suite featured mahogany Louis XV furniture with metal fittings, and the fourth-floor suite was furnished with Louis XVI mahogany pieces and French gray walls.

For visiting dignitaries, there were three state suites with three rooms each. They were designed in such a way that they could be enlarged to include four or five rooms. The Colonial Suite was designed to take visitors back in time as they stepped through the door, with carpets, mural decorations, woodwork and furniture all reflecting colonial style. A massive, mahogany four-poster bed with curtains was the centerpiece of the room.

Named in honor of the "Oleander City," the Oleander Suite was painted a delicate shade of green and bordered with oleander blossoms. Sweeping curves of the white enameled furniture were accented with hand-painted crimson oleander blossoms, and even the Wilton velvet carpet pattern was interwoven with the blooms. The Sheraton Suite was appropriately named for the neoclassical English style of mahogany furniture it featured, with tapered legs and satinwood inlays.

View of east side of Hotel Galvez, 1911.

Wicker roller chairs in front of Hotel Galvez, 1911.

Furniture for the distinctive suites was purchased through the local Kauffman Meyers & Company furniture store, which immediately ran advertisements after the open house offering some of the same pieces to its customers.

At the time Hotel Galvez opened, part of the strategy to make Galveston the "Atlantic City of the South" was to offer roller chairs as an amusing means to travel along the seawall. A group of island businessmen who had visited the East Coast town brought back positive accounts of their popularity, seeing them as a novelty that would be of great interest to tourists.

The Galvez Wheel Chair Company, owned by Charles P. Magill and Frank A. Allen, opened its office at the Hotel Galvez. The custom-ordered chairs began arriving in Galveston in time for the grand opening. Considered an improvement over the East Coast version, the two-wheeled chairs were constructed of willow and designed to carry either one or two people while being pushed by another. Passengers would ride beneath a fringed silk sunshade above the chair and enjoy the Gulf breeze and views, while an attendant pushed the vehicle along a four-mile stretch of the boulevard.

Working in conjunction with the hotel, the company rented the conveyances to guests and other visitors throughout the summer months. During special events such as the Cotton Carnival, one-way roller-chair

Above: East loggia sun parlor, 1911.

Left: Loggia view facing west with opened windows, circa 1911.

rides were given from the Galvez to the carnival for twenty-five cents or from the bathhouse to the carnival for fifteen cents.

Additional conveniences available to guests were a Western Union Telegraph office, phone booths, a branch of the United States Post Office and a livery office.

The Hotel Galvez even made special arrangements to obtain a sample room on the Strand in the business district that could be used by traveling salesmen guests to display and sell their wares. Despite this luxury, many salesmen received customers in their hotel rooms at the Galvez and ran newspaper advertisements listing their room numbers.

12

CHINA AND SILVER

Every detail was taken into consideration to create an elegant environment at the Hotel Galvez, and the service ware was no exception.

The trademark oleander theme utilized throughout the hotel appeared on the signature china as well, along with the crest of Bernardo de Gálvez. Rimmed with the attractive pink blooms, this glazed service ware was used in the Marine Restaurant and for buffets and banquets. It was created especially for Hotel Galvez at the Villeroy & Boch factory in Mettlach, Germany, for the durable hotel line of Burley & Company of Chicago. The firm also supplied customized china to at least six railroads beginning in 1891 and the Cloverleaf Steamboat Line on Lake Erie around 1900.

Some of the pieces, such as the spittoon shown in the accompanying image, were manufactured as part of the Chester Hotel China line by the Taylor, Smith & Taylor Company of West Virginia. This particular flat-bottomed, weighted style was known as a Chester Spittoon and was designed specifically for use by hotels and saloons. It was most likely used in the Galvez's gentlemen's club. Provided in an effort to reduce public spitting of tobacco on floors, spittoons, or cuspidors, were common sights at high-end hotels, railcars, saloons and banks.

Silver service pieces for the Hotel Galvez were personally selected by Jack Letton. Furnished by the Galveston firm of M.O. Nobbe & Company, a local jewelry and optics house, they were designed and manufactured by Gorham of New York. Invoices received for the 7,988 separate pieces of silverware ordered required six typewritten sheets to specify all of the categories.

Top, left: Original 1911 ceramic plate from Hotel Galvez restaurant service.

Top, right: Original 1911 ceramic spittoon from the Hotel Galvez gentlemen's parlor.

Bottom: Unusual silver souvenir demitasse spoon with etching of Hotel Galvez and full-figure Indian, by Let 'Er Buck, circa 1911. *Author's collection.*

There was such interest about the extravagant set in the community that on May 29, 1910, just two weeks before it was put into use, Nobbe & Co. invited the public to an open house at its store to see the complete silver service displayed "in all of its magnificent brilliance." Among the included items were a seemingly unending array of covered plates, tiny demitasse spoons, champagne buckets, coffee pots, small chafing dishes, 864 coffee spoons, 576 oyster forks, lobster forks, extra long iced-tea spoons, coffee sets, ice-cream dishes, bread trays, butter dishes, sauce boats and tiny sets of gold-topped shakers for salt, pepper and paprika.

The hotel's superintendent of service was on hand from 8:00 p.m. to 10:00 p.m. to answer questions as the curious visitors filed through the exhibit, which took the staff of the store three hours to set out. The piece that received the most inquiries by intrigued visitors was a uniquely French invention, the duck press. Each piece was tastefully simple and ornamented with a deeply engraved Galvez coat of arms.

Nobbe would open a second shop on the first floor of the Galvez, offering jewelry and exclusive souvenirs such as spoons, pin trays and powder compacts emblazoned with the image of Hotel Galvez.

Examples of the hotel's service ware including china, silver and crystal, can be seen in the basement-level history displays at the Hotel Galvez today. Original service pieces from the Hotel Galvez china are highly valued among collectors.

13

HOLIDAYS AND PARTIES

It's difficult to imagine the countless number of celebrations that have taken place at the Hotel Galvez in over one hundred years: wedding parties, ladies' luncheons, debutante balls, holiday parties, Mardi Gras festivities, convention banquets, reunions, award presentations and more.

Here is just a sampling of some of the fantastic events that have been hosted at the Galvez.

Bal Poudre 1911

Robert Waverly Smith and his wife, Jenny, entertained guests at a Bal Poudre, or "powdered wig ball," in the ballroom of the Hotel Galvez in December 1911.

The French eighteenth-century themed gala was given in honor of Miss Fowler and Miss McVitie, daughters of prominent businessmen on the island. Decorations for the event were said to have transformed the appearance of the hotel to such a degree that guests gasped in delight as they entered.

As the event was held the night after Christmas, many of the decorations incorporated traditional holiday elements.

Conway Rollin Shaw's orchestra played from the balcony, referred to as the "musicians' gallery," which was decked with masses of holly.

Large Christmas trees illuminated with tiny incandescent bulbs nestled in their boughs stood at the north end of the ballroom, adorned with hundreds

Ladies' luncheon in the Galvez Club during the National Hotel Convention, 1957. *Courtesy of the Moody Family Archives.*

of brightly colored ornaments. Surrounding the trees were toys, which would be given as favors during the cotillions. These gifts were artistically arranged in rows to create an attractive vignette with dolls in back of groupings of drums and horns tied with wide red ribbons. A mass of fuzzy, stuffed dogs and velvet cats waited at the bases of the trees for their turn to be presented to young guests as well.

Holly wreaths with red tulle bows hung against the lace window curtains, and garlands and boughs of smilax, mistletoe and holly were draped above doorways and between pillars.

The terraces on either side of the ballroom were enclosed and draped with greenery and flags, providing softly lit conversation areas during dance intermissions.

As stunning as the decorations for the gathering were, they did not command the same admiration earned by guests' costumes. Looking as if they had stepped directly out of antique oil paintings, attendees spared no expense in arriving in the finest period fashions.

In keeping with the theme of the ball, guests wore old-fashioned powdered white wigs. Gentlemen wore knickerbockers and lace jabots, and

Main ballroom with musicians' balcony, 1911.

many adorned their costumes with courtly decorations with faux gemstones suspended by ribbons.

Ladies delighted in wearing various styles of wigs, some with loose curls and others spun in high Marie Antoinette fashion. Feathers or blossoms that coordinated with their ball gowns accented the hairstyles. Nearly all of the women carried old-fashioned nosegays with paper accents.

Satin gowns of white, lavender, blue and rose pink swirled around the dance floor during the night's four cotillions, three of which were led by Charles Hillenbrand and the remaining one by William R.A. Rogers with Miss Terry.

After the second cotillion, the attendees promenaded to dinner in the Terrace Dining Room. Tartan stockings filled with gifts for the boys and girls hung from large butterfly bows of red gauze on the back of each chair, and pop caps and table favors added to the fun.

The final two cotillions took place after the meal.

Charming favors were presented to the guests after each cotillion, such as ivory-spangled gauze fans with ribbons for the ladies and leather bill cases and brush cases for the gentlemen.

Dance programs ornamented with a gold-and-blue monogram of the host and hostess served as additional souvenirs of the unusual evening.

New Year's Eve 1911

The first New Year's Eve event was so well received that it virtually took over the ground floor of the Galvez to accommodate musicians, dancing and dining space for four hundred guests.

The Matus Royal Hungarian Court Orchestra began to serenade attendees in the lobby and mezzanine balcony at 9:00 p.m.; an hour later, the doors to the event formally opened, inviting guests to walk beneath a greenery archway topped with "1912" displayed in electric lights.

Each guest was issued a number to a corresponding table place card at tables filling the east wing of the Galvez, encompassing the corridors and both dining rooms. Favors, such as ladies' engagement books, were left on each plate, in addition to the assorted festive trinkets strewn along the tablecloths.

Individual programs for the evening were printed on the hotel's press. The front covers were decorated with hand-painted pictures appropriate for the occasion, with the dinner menu and music program on the inside. Blank space was left inside the pamphlet to collect signatures of friends and make notes about the experience, creating a memento of the evening.

As the midnight hour approached, guests spotted a ball hanging from the mezzanine floor with an attendant nearby, mimicking a tradition that began in New York's Times Square four years earlier.

The room lights dimmed, and each of the first six bell tolls marked strokes of the midnight hour until the entire wing was in utter darkness, adding to the excitement. The last six strokes sounded, and a large electrified sign proclaiming "1912" was lighted at the balcony, causing the crowd to burst into applause. The lighting in the room was then returned, and the merriment and dancing continued for hours.

This was the first of many New Year's celebrations at the hotel.

Flag Raising 1913

Even the simplest occasion became the inspiration for celebration at the Galvez, so when a new, seventy-five-foot-tall flagpole was erected on the grounds in the fall of 1913, plans were busily made.

Taking part in the hotel's first flag-raising ceremony on October 2 were Colonel Daniel Cornman, commanding the Fifth Brigade, Second Division of the United States Army, then at Galveston, along with Colonel Millard F. Waltz, commanding the Nineteenth Infantry, his entire regiment and the regimental band.

The Galvez balconies were opened to the public to provide unobstructed views of the ceremony, since participating soldiers occupied the driveways and lawns.

Colonel Waltz and his staff took their position in front of the south entrance and commanded the regiment, which was divided into three battalions facing east, west and south surrounding the flagpole. After the band played several numbers for the crowd, Waltz gave a signal, and the flag was carried to the site.

Mrs. David Lauber, wife of the manager of the Galvez at the time, accompanied by two noncommissioned officers, raised the colors to the peak of the flagstaff. The regiment presented arms, and the flag waved above the courtyard to the strains of "The Star-Spangled Banner."

Colonel Waltz, the members of his staff and the brigade commanders were guests at a dinner given by the Laubers at the Galvez on the evening of the flag raising.

A clever miniature replica of the afternoon's event served as a table decoration, with a four-foot flagpole stationed in the center of the table. Evergreens and American Beauty roses surrounded the base of the pole and, after the guests were seated, soft rose-colored lights concealed in the arrangement were turned on.

Before the meal was served, Colonel Waltz hoisted the miniature silk flag to the top of the pole, while the Hotel Galvez Orchestra played "The Star-Spangled Banner."

A dance was given after the dinner for officers of the U.S. Army encamped in Galveston and the surrounding area, which was attended by about 250 couples, in a ballroom that had been patriotically decorated for the event.

Halloween 1913

In 1913, Hotel Galvez was the scene of a Halloween dinner dance that has become somewhat legendary on the island for its extravagance. Over three hundred guests arrived in costume on Friday, October 31, to attend one of the largest social gatherings of the season.

Dinner was served in the Terrace Dining Room and east corridor of the hotel, both of which had been transformed into a mystic, picturesque setting. Large yellow pumpkins sat atop banks of straw that circled the Terrace Room, and large stalks of corn were stacked about decorated with witches, pumpkins and jack-o-lanterns. Garlands of moss were draped from the chandeliers and columns, making the space feel more a home for goblins than hotel visitors.

Lighted electric globes with shades resembling miniature pumpkins brightened the dining tables, which were decorated with immense yellow chrysanthemums in crystal vases and place cards painted with designs of jack-o-lanterns, goblins, witches and pumpkins.

Following the dinner, a costume dance was given in the ballroom of the Galvez with music provided by the Nineteenth Infantry Band, and a silver trophy was awarded to the winners of the costume contest.

Guests included some of the local citizens who were credited with helping the Galvez come into existence, including Mr. and Mrs. E.O. Flood, Mr. and Mrs. W.L. Moody and Mr. and Mrs. Robert Cohen

New Year's Eve 1913

That same year, just months before the beginning of World War I, a unique military-themed New Year's Eve ball was hosted by the hotel to welcome in 1914 as a reflection of the enthusiastic patriotism at the time.

The Twenty-Eighth Infantry Orchestra performed popular dance tunes from 9:00 p.m. to 11:00 p.m., when a "mess call" was sounded on bugles signaling the celebratory troops of guests to adjourn to dinner. The colonnade leading to the dining rooms was converted into an Italian garden with smilax covering the walls and a canopy of miniature red roses arched overhead.

The Terrace Dining Room was most ornately decorated with garlands of smilax and studded with rose electric lamps, and the chandeliers were fashioned after poinsettias with red draping. Red globes enclosed all of the electric lights on the first floor, in honor of the color shared by the holidays and the American flag.

As the hand of the clock neared 12:00 a.m., hidden bugles played taps as a farewell to 1913, followed by an Oriental gong that slowly boomed the strokes of the hour as midnight arrived. When the last one sounded, a flashing marque announcing "1914" lighted the room.

The military band played "The Star-Spangled Banner" to bring in the New Year, and a standing toast was given before celebrants returned to the party.

Artillery Ball 1913

The 1913 ball of the Galveston Artillery Club, a private members group, resembled an exotic night in the Orient. This event, or one with almost identical decor, was featured on a popular postcard of the hotel.

The ballroom's ivory woodwork with gold accents and sparkling chandeliers harmonized beautifully with decorative Asian accents that included groupings of electrified Japanese lanterns suspended from ropes of smilax strung back and forth across the width of the ballroom, providing a soft glow over the space. Brightly colored paper Japanese-style parasols were inverted and suspended between the greenery.

During intermissions between dances, guests rested in the ivory willow furniture of the loggia and east and west terraces hung with smilax and flowers and ornamented with potted palms and ferns, giving the effect of sitting in a tropical garden. Silk-draped candelabra provided intimate, soft lighting for the guests. It must have seemed like a brief excursion to a faraway land.

In addition to decades of special events, the Hotel Galvez offered distinctive lunches and dinners for most major holidays, including Easter and Mother's Day brunches that, to this day, are two of the most popular food-related events on the island.

Hotel Galvez ballroom decorated with Japanese parasols and lanterns, 1913. *Author's collection.*

Left: Thanksgiving dinner advertisement, 1918. *Author's collection.*

Above: Christmas Day dinner advertisement, 1920. *Author's collection.*

Stella's Orchestra often performed at parties and special events at Hotel Galvez.

HOTEL GALVEZ

SITUATED on Famous Seawall, overlooking Beautiful Gulf of Mexico, within stone throw of the finest surf bathing in the world, offers a charming and ideal retreat for those seeking pleasure, recreation and health. Its location affords the convenience of a Metropolis, without its attendant annoyances, being within easy walking distance of the Galveston shopping center and railway stations, and yet, far enough removed from the hubbub of traffic to be entirely free from disturbing noises.

European Plan

Rates { Rooms, for 1 person, $2.00 } Per Day and
{ Rooms, for 2 persons, 3.00 } Upwards

Left and next two pages: Hotel Galvez marketing brochure, 1915.

U. S. TRANSPORTS DOCKED AT GALVESTON

APPOINTMENTS

HOTEL GALVEZ is a magnificent six story fire-proof structure of 250 rooms, built in the Spanish mission style of architecture, at a cost of more than One Million Dollars. Its appointments combine comfort, refined elegance and convenience to a high degree. The spacious lobby, broad loggia with inviting easy chairs, roomy sun parlor and grand ball room overlooking the Gulf, invite indolence with the outspoken assurance of satisfying comfort and contentment.

LOGGIA, HOTEL GALVEZ

DINING ROOM

PLAYGROUND OF THE SOUTHWEST, PANORAMIC VIEW OF HOTEL GALVEZ, BOULEVARD, SEAWALL AND BEACH

BATHING AT GALVESTON

GALVESTON'S Beach is justly famed for the excellence of its surf bathing. Overlooked by a sea wall seventeen feet high, five miles long and entirely free from debris, the Galveston Beach is a playground of unusual attractiveness. A number of commodious bathing pavilions within view of Hotel Galvez insure the comfort and convenience of all who wish to play in the sea. Bathing may be indulged in here practically all year round, and it is at its height from April 1st to November 1st.

SPEEDWAY—30 MILES OF BEACH FRONT

A SINGLE DAY'S CATCH

BATHING PAVILIONS,
BOULEVARD AND SEAWALL

CUISINE

HOTEL GALVEZ enjoys an enviable reputation for the excellence of its cuisine and elegant appointments of its spacious dining rooms, terrace out-door restaurant and Japanese tea room. An infinite variety of seafoods, fresh from the water, rare fruits and garden delicacies found only in semi-tropical climates, make possible the preparation of many tempting dishes not to be found elsewhere.

PALM GARDEN, GALVESTON

OLEANDER TREE IN BLOOM

OTHER ATTRACTIONS

GUESTS of Hotel Galvez may have the use of the Oleander Country Club's Golf Links and Club Rooms.

A thirty-mile beach drive—60 miles with one turn—on the very fringe of the Gulf affords the autoist a delightful speedway.

All out door sports—Tennis, Riding, Driving, Motoring, Fishing, Hunting, Boating.

Ideal climate, pleasant environment and friendly hospitality—combined with all the comforts and luxuries known to modern hotels, make Hotel Galvez an ideal place to spend a vacation.

You are cordially invited to write for any information that may be helpful in planning your vacation.

DAVID LAUBER, Manager,
The Home of the Tarpon.   Galveston, Texas.

SOUTH VIEW OF BALL ROOM

Hundreds of performers, bands and orchestras from around the world played at these special events and concerts through the years. Some of the most popular were the Carl Singer, Charles Coverman and Seth Abergh Trio, Sara Helen Littlejohn, military bands, Conway Rollin Shaw and the Felix Stella Orchestra.

14

1915 HURRICANE

Though the 1900 Storm receives most of the weather-related attention historically for Galveston due to the devastation and loss of life it caused, another, stronger hurricane followed it in August 1915, just four years after the opening of the Hotel Galvez. The category 4 hurricane put the construction of the city's seawall and grand hotel to the ultimate test.

In the days prior to the storm, the Conference of Southern Bankers had taken place in Galveston, and many of the attendees and their families had extended their stay to enjoy vacation time on the island. Though the conference ended on Saturday and warnings were already being issued to the community, visitors viewed the coming storm as a curiosity.

Galveston's local weather bureau notified the public on Saturday to move from low-lying areas to higher ground behind the seawall. The barrier had withstood previous storms, such as a 1909 hurricane, when a storm surge of ten feet came ashore, causing the deaths of five Galvestonians, none of whom were behind the seawall. These early warnings are credited with protecting hundreds of lives, giving Galvestonians and visitors time to either evacuate or seek safer housing.

By Saturday evening, the rough surf discouraged bathers from entering the water and people gradually cleared the beaches. The following morning, conditions had worsened considerably.

Hotel Galvez, considered one of the most substantial buildings, sheltered hundreds of its own guests, residents who had left their homes and visitors

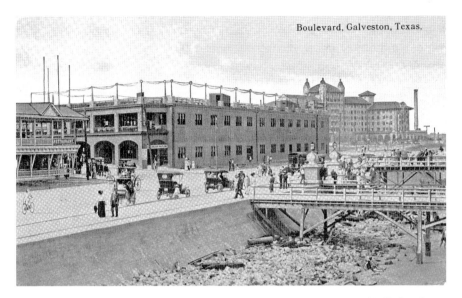

Brown Casino, in forefront of photo, offered a skating rink, dance hall, pool hall, shooting gallery and ice-cream parlor, circa 1912. *Author's collection.*

who left smaller motels seeking more substantial protection. Every room was occupied, and people were asked to share rooms with others in order to accommodate everyone who applied for space. Late arrivals stayed in the lobby and other gathering areas.

The hurricane hit Galveston on Monday, August 16, with the worse intensity arriving after midnight. The winds and rain continued to pound the island for three more days, twice as long as the Great Storm had lasted.

True to its purpose, the concave face of the seawall diminished the force of the waves by redirecting their energy upward and back toward the surf. Though the full force of the water was deflected, strong winds whipped across the top of the wall, throwing the edges of the sea spray against the Galvez with enough force to shatter windows up to the fifth floor.

Galvez manager David Lauber and assistant manager Phillip Luther Sanders and their staff worked throughout the night, making everyone as comfortable as possible, but several women fainted, children cried and men were visibly uneasy. Several adults took charge of the situation by distracting children with games and songs. Once they had settled into the activities, the grown-ups calmed down as well.

The Hotel Galvez Orchestra played music as the storm intensified; soon, groups of young men and women began to dance. It was quite possibly the first example of a hurricane party on record.

A.C. Owsley, who was visiting from Denton with his young son Henry, watched what he described as the "magnificent spectacle" of the storm from the dining porch of the Hotel Galvez. He later told his hometown newspaper that the guests of the Galvez, along with hundreds of others, remained outdoors, some standing atop the seawall, watching the fury of the storm. When the winds increased in strength and tore away part of the roof of the porch and whisked off tables and chairs, they were convinced to seek safety inside.

Guests watched through windows as fires broke out at a nearby laundry and packinghouse and smoke rose from distant parts of the city.

Witnesses at the Galvez observed the storm as its energy broke across the top of the seawall with such force that two granite monuments placed at the foot of Tremont Street to commemorate the construction of the seawall were torn from their bases and heaved across the boulevard, a distance of more than fifty feet. Visitors today can see these monuments, now back in their proper place, to get a sense of how powerful the hurricane had to have been to move them.

Electricity, telephone and telegraph services were lost at 5:00 p.m. on Monday as the force of the storm was breaking on the island, and the Galvez utilized candles as sources of light. The kitchen suspended room

The 1915 hurricane's damage to roadway on top of Galveston's seawall, with Hotel Galvez in the background.

service when the electricity failed, requiring those who had remained in their rooms to come into the main rooms of the hotel for food.

Merchants in the business district continued the work of moving their merchandise to places of safety, but by 9:00 p.m., depths of water on Market Street of four to six feet forced them to abandon their efforts.

During the height of the storm, a four-masted schooner named the *Dora Allison* was thrust into the seawall at the foot of Thirty-Ninth Street. It was dragging two anchors, which caught under the foot of the barrier, preventing its escape. Caught in place, the ship was reportedly dashed to pieces after being repeatedly buffeted against the wall. The fact that the collision only knocked off two chips of the wall, about two cubic feet, was a testament to the strength of its design and construction.

From the first rough surf to the last of the rainfall, Galveston remained in the hurricane zone for a staggering 153 hours.

The Hotel Galvez sheltered thousands of people and fed hundreds for two days without charge. Though the water was two inches deep in the dining room, "bread lines" were formed to distribute food and drink to anyone who requested it. The kitchen and waitstaff served potatoes and other small items for lunch and more substantial food for dinner. Coffee and bread were served throughout the night and the next day. On Wednesday morning, the hotel went back to charging for food, including a reasonably priced breakfast of coffee, three rolls and butter for twenty-five cents.

Lieutenant Max Wainer and his wife, Amy Elvin Wainer, had been staying at the hotel through all the excitement. On August 20, while the hotel staff was busily getting back into their normal routines, Amy gave birth to a little boy, Max Jr., in Room 231. The manager of the Galvez wrote a letter of congratulations to the couple, assuring them that the hotel would take care of them during the remainder of their stay. The letter has been passed down in the family as a cherished memento of the special day and circumstances.

Once the storm passed, the work of cleaning up and getting the hotel back in order began.

The lovely gardens surrounding the grounds had been ruined, but the seawall had protected the Galvez from major harm. Water had brought silt and dirt into the first floor, ruining the carpets; the basement filled with water; sections of the tile roof were missing; and windows had been broken. The damage amounted to approximately $10,000 to $15,000.

Not every business fared as well. Murdoch's, the Breakers and the Surf bathhouses and the fishing piers were in ruins, and large sections of the brick boulevard along the seawall were washed away, leaving the bricks in

The 1915 storm's damage along seawall, with Hotel Galvez on the right.

Hotel Galvez from seawall showing brick-paved streets, circa 1915.

piles. It was even reported that the currency in every bank had sustained water damage.

An official representative of the city confirmed to news agencies, "Practically all the houses east of Twentieth and near [Seawall] boulevard were destroyed." Roughly 90 percent of the homes on Galveston Island outside of the seawall's protection were lost.

The greatest structural loss for the city was the new $2 million causeway. The center arch was all that remained after the winds caused a horrific collapse, cutting off traffic between Galveston and the mainland. Guests of the Galvez anxious to return to the mainland were able to ride in a tugboat to Texas City on Thursday and take a train from the station there.

By the following week, even with repairs underway, the Hotel Galvez began running advertisements in the local newspapers that visitors could expect "business as usual" when coming to the hotel. There was outdoor dining at tables on the lawn and terrace, dancing during dinners on Tuesdays and Fridays and weekly "Hops" (casual dances) on Saturdays and Thursdays. The kitchen operations had returned to normal, and a special dinner on the terrace was held on August 29 with music and singing.

In 1916, Isaac Kempner, one of the original Galvez "Fathers," was elected chairman of the Citizens Committee to rebuild the causeway, which stood for railway use through the next fifty years of storms.

15

PAGEANT OF PULCHRITUDE

In 1920, thanks to a marketing campaign spearheaded by the Galveston Beach Association, the number of visitors to island beaches was larger than ever. They came for the sand and water, but also for special attractions like Oakley Aerial Escadrille, which performed airplane stunts over the beach. Other events included horse races, motorcycle races, car shows, airplane races and fireworks displays. The Hotel Galvez, perfectly positioned for close access to the events, also held free band concerts on the front lawn courtesy of the association.

Without a doubt the most exciting event in Galveston that year was the Galveston Beach Bathing Girl Revue, which eventually inspired an annual tradition that made the Galvez its headquarters. A full-page advertisement in the *Galveston Daily News* invited young ladies to "help us make it an artistic success," promising a grand prize of a $250 diamond ring. In addition to the beauty contest, there would be diamond ring and lavaliere prizes for Most Elaborate Costume, Most Original Costume, Most Becoming Costume, Most Unique Costume and Most Artistic Costume. There were even "Baby Divisions" for boys and girls ages two to six, with cash prizes.

The organizers elected local newspapermen from the *Houston Post*, *Houston Chronicle*, *Galveston Tribune* and *Galveston News* to act as judges, virtually guaranteeing widespread news coverage for the day.

Cohen's Department Store capitalized on the event, advertising everything contestants might need to be a winning mermaid: bathing suits, bathing caps, bathing shoes, bathing hosiery, rubberized bags, bathing garters, beach

SCENE SHOWING GALVESTON'S FAMOUS AUTOMOBILE BEACH RACE COURSE.

ANOTHER SCENE OF THE FAMOUS AUTOMOBILE BEACH RACE COURSE.

Top: Automobile races on Galveston Beach, circa 1914.

Bottom: Hotel Galvez with Joyland Park and crowded seawall in the foreground, circa 1919.

wraps, bathing sports coats, bathing belts, swimming wings, beach costumes, bathing corsets and beach parasols.

As if a parade of beauties would not be enough to draw a crowd, the committee hired Dare Devil Frank LeRoy, "King of the High Wire," to perform twice daily on Saturday and Sunday on a tightwire stretched from the roof of the Crystal Palace to an adjoining roof. It was also opening day for Joyland Park's Great American Derby Racing, a $45,000 carousel on the seawall.

Contestants in the 1923 Pageant of Pulchritude, posing in front of the Hotel Galvez.

Those thrilled with the possibility of appearing on film were delighted to hear that Pathe News was scheduled to shoot newsreels of all the special events.

The Hotel Galvez and other hotels had record guest bookings for the year, as many of the twenty thousand people who arrived to watch the revue decided to stay for the weekend. Numerous Houstonians purchased round-trip tickets on the Sunday excursion train for a mere $1.65 each.

Over fifty contestants donned their finest bathing costumes on May 23 for their chance to take home the coveted winner's sash and prizes. Beginning at the roof garden of the Crystal Palace, an elaborate three-story bathhouse and entertainment venue, contestants strolled along a temporary boardwalk constructed on the riprap at the foot of the seawall. After reaching the east end fishing pier, they returned to the Palace while being cheered on by the crowds. The ladies were judged on "general attractiveness, originality and becomingness."

Reba Dick of Galveston was awarded the grand prize, wearing a scarlet costume, red silk accordion pleated cape and ribbon bathing cap. She carried a scarlet parasol to complete the triumphant outfit. Karen Dufty won the category of Most Elaborate Costume with an orange-and-black butterfly costume with a gauze butterfly atop her head and a parasol of tulle.

The term *Miss Universe* was first used in 1926, when the Seventh Annual Bathing Revue adopted the name of the International Pageant of Pulchritude, with "pulchritude" being an elaborate word meaning "beauty." Though most of the thirty-nine entries came from Texas and surrounding states as in previous years of the revue, the participation of contestants Miss Mexico Maria Martha Parres from Mexico and Patricia

O'Shea from Winnipeg made the competition Galveston's first true international event.

Some of the contestants not accustomed to sunny climates incurred burns and blisters during the swimsuit parades, while others carried parasols to shade themselves.

Though reportedly around 160,000 people watched the opening parade of the ladies in their bathing suits that year, costumes, props and "other decorations" were not considered in the judging process that focused on beauty, form, grace and personal charm. The pageant itself was held the following day.

Prizes were awarded at the American Beauty Ball on May 17 at the Garden of Tokio, an open-air dancing pavilion next door to the Galvez, beneath crystal chandeliers, Japanese lanterns and thousands of colored electric lights.

Catherine Moylan, Miss Dallas, won the $2,000 grand prize, becoming the first Beauty Queen of the Universe. She went on to become an actress, starring in movies such as *Love in the Rough*, *Our Blushing Brides* and *Any Old Port*.

The second-place winner received $1,000, the third $250 and the remaining nine places received $100 each.

Rosebud Blondell from Dallas may have been disappointed to place twelfth in the competition, but she went on to have a long, successful career in Hollywood under the name Joan Blondell.

Contestants and their chaperones who participated in the Second International Pageant of Pulchritude in May 1927 were provided with accommodations at the Hotel Galvez for the duration of the three-day event.

Aerial view of the Hotel Galvez, circa 1920.

An estimated 250,000 people attended the events during that weekend. In addition to over $5,000 in prizes, the pageant was also becoming known as an opportunity for potential movie and stage actresses to be discovered.

The contest was changed this year by dividing it into two separate events. Gaido's Restaurant treated the beauties to lunch on the first day, before the popular swimsuit parade along the seawall accompanied by several bands. Later that evening, the contestants were invited to a dance aboard the pleasure boat *Galvez*.

On the following morning, only American entrants, coming from as far away as New York and Utah, would vie for the title of Miss United States. An afternoon pageant included the newly crowned Miss United States in competition against the international participants, including those from England, Russia, Turkey, Austria, Egypt, Thailand, Philippines, Hong Kong, Japan and Brazil. The winner of this second pageant would be crowned Beauty Queen of the Universe.

Dorothy Britton, Miss New York, was awarded both titles, attributing her win, in part, to wearing a locket with her mother's photo throughout the event. The achievement earned Britton $2,000 in gold, a silver plaque engraved "Beauty Queen of the Universe" and a twelve-week tour of personal appearances.

In 1928, there were forty-two contestants (thirty-two American and ten foreign) in the Third Annual International Pageant of Pulchritude. Miss Chicago, Ella Van Hueson, was crowned Miss Universe and took home the grand prize of $2,000. The second-place winner received $1,000, the third-place winner $250 and the remaining nine places received $100 each.

The event grew in size in 1929, and an estimated one hundred thousand cheering spectators stood along the parade route as cars brought the American and international contestants through the streets of the city to the Hotel Galvez. Participants, their chaperones and seven celebrity judges including Galveston-born Hollywood director King Vidor were provided with rooms at the Galvez for the event. The pageant was praised in the media for its moral tone, noting that improper talk or actions among the entrants were nonexistent.

After a full day of activities and competitions, the beauties returned to their rooms, passing through a lobby filled with admirers.

The chamber of commerce gave a grand testimonial banquet for all the entrants and their chaperones in the Terrace Dining Room of the Hotel Galvez, where prizes and the title of Miss Universe were officially awarded. The grand prize winner, Miss Austria, was given $2,000 in gold and a silver plaque engraved with her new title.

Winners of the pageant gathered on the grounds of the Hotel Galvez the following morning to pose for a throng of photographers and newsreel film crews. That night, the winner and a panel of judges dined at the Galvez once again as guests of the Galveston Rotary Club.

The 1930 pageant year was more glamorous than any before it, with five days of events from August 2 to 6. National and international media covered the contestants' every move. The contestants were invited to a Beauty Ball at the Galvez to welcome them on their first night on the island. The following day, after photos and interviews, there was a bathing suit parade at 5:00 p.m., and the girls were introduced in their evening gowns at 9:00 p.m.

The stunning winner this year, Dorothy Dell, became one of the most famous participants to appear in the pageant. After winning the title of Miss New Orleans at the age of seventeen in 1930, Dell went on to be crowned Miss Universe at the Pageant of Pulchritude the same year. Within a few short months, Florenz Ziegfeld saw one of her singing performances and hired her for the renowned Ziegfeld Follies on Broadway. She then signed a contract with Paramount Pictures and starred in movies including *Little Miss*

Marker with Shirley Temple. Tragically, she lost her life in an automobile accident at the age of nineteen.

An unusually "modern" young lady won the title the following year. A tall, green-eyed brunette named Netta Duchâteau was the very first Miss Belgium, and her participation in the 1931 pageant captured the admiration of the judges' panel. During the famous street parade, in which the swimsuit-clad beauties road through the streets of the city introducing themselves to city officials, nineteen-year-old Netta managed to charm everyone despite the fact that she did not speak a word of English.

The intelligent young lady was also highly praised for her ability to fly airplanes, having earned a license in her home country. Flying was thought to be a courageous act for a woman. Her combination of beauty and brains earned her the Miss Universe crown, to the delight of onlookers.

Before and after a farewell banquet held for girls, mothers and newspapermen by the chamber of commerce at the Hotel Galvez, visitors stopped in to get a glimpse of the contestants relaxing in the lounge of the hotel.

Tourists on beach and seawall in front of Hotel Galvez, circa 1920.

White plastic souvenir fan with images of Galveston, Hotel Galvez and a ferryboat, circa 1920.

Galveston's seaside contest, the predecessor to the Miss Universe Pageant, attracted enough spectators at the height of its success to triple the island's population during the event. The annual parade of beauties in fanciful costumes, sometimes walking, sometimes riding floats or in automobiles along lines of cheering crowds, announced the official start of the summer season.

Each year, official panoramic photographs were taken of contestants lined up in their swimwear. These have become sought-after collectibles to this day.

Sadly, the pageant was discontinued in 1932 due to the Great Depression and the impending threat of events leading up to World War II. Galveston Bishop Christopher Edward Byrne may have been the only one to take joy in the end of the tradition, having waged a long fight against the "leg show on the seawall."

The spirit of the beauty pageant era lives on in Galveston in the form of the Galveston Island Beach Revue, which began in 2009. Local contestants, many wearing 1920s- and 1930s-style swimwear and retro clothing, take part in reviving this fun piece of history every year for appreciative onlookers.

16

BAKER HOTELS

Tourism was entering a renewed boom era for the island. Local attractions increased each year, luring visitors from near and far, and transportation was no longer an issue.

A high-speed Interurban line linked Houston with Galveston from 1911 to 1936, making the fifty-mile trip from downtown to downtown in only seventy-five minutes. The Houston Electric Streetcar Line and Galveston-Houston Electric Railway shared tracks across a concrete causeway carrying happy day-trippers to the business district or beach. Passengers often boarded and detrained a short walk from the Twenty-First Street entrance of Hotel Galvez.

Galveston found great success as a destination for conventions, as well; in 1923 alone, it hosted more than thirty-six.

In 1928, the Baker Corporation, owners of multiple hotels in Texas, purchased the Galvez from its original owners, and it opened under the Baker umbrella in November of that year. At the time of the sale, the hotel company petitioned to have Twentieth Street closed to traffic between Avenue P and the seawall. The section remains closed to this day.

Tom Moore, the hotel's new manager, undertook a modernization program, restructuring the restaurants and operations of the Galvez.

Visitors at the time could enjoy a seventy-five-cent luncheon that included their choice of roast leg of veal or mutton, celery dressing, green pea soup, buttered squash, French fried potatoes, ginger ale fruit salad and hot mince pie. Guests lounging in the loggia or playing shuffleboard on the lawn sipped

The Texas Limited train, which ran between Galveston and Houston, 1911–36.

Boardwalk in front of Hotel Galvez, circa 1930.

on martinis, Gibsons and Artillery Triangles (a mixture of gin, vermouth and Dubonnet) or tropical daiquiris for twenty cents.

William Lewis Moody Jr. built the $1 million Buccaneer Hotel on the seawall in 1929, two blocks east of the Galvez. The eleven-story hotel offered "modern" facilities and presented competition for tourists.

In 1931, the gentlemen who originally formed the Hotel Galvez Company appointed Mayor Jack E. Pearce as a trustee and bought back the Galvez from Baker Interests. The Hotel Galvez Operating Company, headed by Isaac Kempner, then repurchased the hotel from Pearce for one dollar, restoring ownership to Galvestonians.

17

TEMPORARY WHITE HOUSE

Not many hotels can claim to have been a temporary White House for a U.S. president, but the Hotel Galvez has that distinctive honor.

During a visit to Washington, D.C., in early 1937, Isaac Kempner was told in confidence by Houston businessman Jesse Jones that President Franklin Delano Roosevelt was planning a ten-day offshore fishing trip to the Texas Gulf Coast. Due to the length of the visit, it would be necessary for a temporary White House to be established either in Houston or Galveston.

"I made appointments with the president's secretary, Colonel Marvin Hunter McIntyre, and the head of the Secret Service who had to approve of all locations," Kempner reminisced in his memoirs. Due to his actions and government connections, Galveston and the Hotel Galvez were approved for use as headquarters.

Of course, a fishing trip by a president of the United States takes a great deal more planning and extraordinary measures than most vacations. Preparations for establishing the temporary White House at the Galvez and maintaining communication between it and the president, who would be onboard a ship, filled the weeks before Roosevelt's arrival.

The hotel and its manager, Paul H. Williams, began the elaborate arrangements to provide adequate quarters for the large group, including supervising the installation of special telephone and telegraph lines. Colonel Edward William Starling and nine Secret Service men arrived on the island in advance of the train to make final plans for the opening of the

WHITE HOUSE — WASHINGTON, D.C.

HOTEL GALVEZ — GALVESTON, TEXAS
Temporary White House May 1st to May 11th, 1937

Galveston's famous beach Hotel selected as Headquarters for White House and Staff during President Roosevelt's fishing trip in the Gulf.

7A-H881

Postcard commemorating Hotel Galvez's temporary White House status. *Author's collection.*

secretarial base, which occupied the entire fifth floor of the Galvez. Williams had already overseen complicated measures to accommodate the group of thirty secretaries, clerks, stenographers and correspondents, including the installation of special telephone and telegraph lines. White House staff occupied Parlor J at the southeast corner of the floor.

The naval destroyer USS *Schenck* was stationed at Pier 21 with a crew of about ninety men, and the U.S. Coast Guard naval radio station on Pelican Spit was given the responsibility of maintaining radio communication. The Coast Guard cutter *Saranac*, which had home ported in Galveston since being commissioned in 1930, left on the morning of April 29 to take a patrolling station along the Texas coast.

Galveston postmaster Robert A. Lyons Jr. was notified that a pouch containing presidential mail would arrive at the municipal airport each day from April 28 through May 9. The postal aircraft arrived on the island each morning and left to return to Washington each evening.

Confidential and sensitive mail addressed to the president required its own exceptional provisions. Herbert G. Theurer, the official postal inspector for President Roosevelt, was personally responsible for all mail received and sent by the president and accompanied him on his travels in the United States and abroad. He supervised the receipt and handling of White House mail through the headquarters at the Hotel Galvez and daily sent it on to the president via two naval seaplanes that arrived in Bolivar Roads several days in advance of the staff. The planes were accompanied by the naval tug USS *Montcalm* for additional security.

On the morning of May 1, 1937, the White House staff arrived at Union Station from New Orleans at 11:50 a.m. on a special Southern Pacific train of eight cars. The group included McIntyre and his wife, Ida; Henry M. Kanee, secretary to McIntyre; Edward W. Smithers, chief telegrapher; W.J. Hopkins, secretary; and Theurer. The entourage also included about forty press representatives, who normally headquartered in the pressroom of the White House. Correspondents from the *New York Herald*, *Wall Street Journal*, *Associated Press*, *New York Times*, *United Press*, *Chicago Tribune*, *International News Service*, *Houston Chronicle* and Western Union were among the reporters and photographers, as well as newsreel crews.

Mayor Adrian F. Levy and city, county and federal officials were at the station to greet the train, in addition to about thirty uniformed police officers. Presidential staff were conveyed from the station to the Hotel Galvez in a caravan of six official city cars escorted by eight motorcycle officers shortly after noon and taken to their offices on the fifth floor.

Galveston, The Treasure Island, "Playground of Texas"   69226

Color linen postcard of Hotel Galvez featuring Murdoch's Pier, Buccaneer Hotel, Speedway Mountain Roller Coaster and aerial performers, circa 1935.

Upon McIntyre's arrival at the Galvez, the hotel officially became the seat of a temporary White House.

Postmaster Lyons, acting on instructions from postal authorities, delivered a large amount of presidential mail to the newly established secretarial office at the Galvez prior to the arrival of the group.

Roosevelt arrived on the coast via the naval destroyer USS *Moffett* and then transferred to the USS *Potomac*. Originally commissioned as the USCG cutter *Electra* in 1934, the *Potomac* had been renamed in 1936 when it began service as the president's official yacht. It was affectionately referred to by the press as the "Floating White House."

Shortly after his staff's arrival at the hotel, a message was received from the president: "Arrived off Aransas Pass at 1:30 this afternoon and commenced fishing. Will spend the night inside jetties. Fog lifted. Lovely afternoon. Further plans on hour to hour basis."

In the true style of southern hospitality, Kempner invited the press correspondents to a garden party at his home that evening, where his wife, Hennie, personally mixed over one hundred mint juleps.

Among the first official business transacted following the establishment of the temporary White House offices was the first unexpected challenge of the staff's stay in Galveston. A new neutrality bill arrived that had been enacted by Congress and required Roosevelt's signature before midnight, when the old neutrality bill expired. Because the two naval seaplanes designated to carry the mail to the yacht had a minor collision the day before and were under repair, Theurer had to take it to Port Aransas by automobile. He arrived at the jetty near where the *Potomac* was anchored, and Roosevelt received and signed the new bill at 6:30 p.m.

Under the watchful protection of the USS *Moffett* and USS *Decatur*, the *Potomac* offered an enjoyable fishing vacation to President Roosevelt. On board with him were Colonel Edwin M. Watson, military aide; Captain Paul Bastedo, naval aide; and Captain Ross T. McIntyre, naval physician to the president. Roosevelt's son Elliott joined the group for the first few days as well before returning home to take care of business matters.

On May 4, McIntyre received a specially built rod and reel at the Hotel Galvez from Harvey H. Haines, vice-president and general manager of the local chamber of commerce. Local sportsmen had contributed money to purchase the gift, which was built by radio technician and local sport fishing authority S. Robert Russell. The design incorporated jeweled movements similar to those used in the finest watches of the day. An offer by a non-Galvestonian to contribute toward the gift was declined by the organizers. The gift was flown by seaplane to the presidential yacht, and a formal presentation speech was made over the radio upon its delivery so that Roosevelt could listen over his headset.

Richard Stringfellow, personal bodyguard to the president, took the opportunity to visit his niece, Galvestonian Kathleen Templin, and her husband, Dr. Sam Templin, when he was off duty during the president's vacation.

Regardless of the enjoyment FDR had fishing the Gulf waters, world events did not stop just because an American president was on vacation. Those few days were no exception. In addition to the neutrality bill that had to be signed, Roosevelt signed thirty-two acts of Congress during his trip to Texas.

On May 6, the *Hindenburg* airship disaster took place in New Jersey, killing thirty-six people. What was planned as one of Germany's latest shows of strength had turned into a national tragedy for the German people. The White House staff and correspondents gathered at the Hotel Galvez as the news was communicated to the presidential party. That evening, the headquarters at the Galvez announced the president's message to Chancellor Adolph Hitler and his expression of sympathy, offering "you and the German people my deepest sympathy for the tragic loss of life." Hitler thanked Roosevelt for the note later in the week. Just a handful of years later, the two countries would be at war.

Elliott returned to Galveston on May 10 and stayed at the Galvez before joining his father for his arrival on the island the next day.

On May 11, after a relaxing eleven days of fishing, Roosevelt's yacht docked in Galveston at 8:00 a.m. to a twenty-one-gun salute from Fort Crockett. Smiling officials greeted him as he disembarked from the *Potomac* at Pier 26, including newly elected congressman Lyndon Baines Johnson, Galveston mayor Adrian Levy and Texas governor James V. Allred.

This was the first meeting of FDR and LBJ and the beginning of a long political and personal relationship. The president invited the congressman to join him as he was driven around the island in Levy's private car. As the motorcade drove past street after street of cheering crowds, the president remarked on the beauty of the island and its oleander-filled esplanades, mentioning that he would like to plant some of the attractive flowers in the White House garden. He also made a special request to see the seawall and peppered Levy with questions about its construction.

The president addressed a crowd of several thousand supporters at a beachfront park, stating that he thought Galveston was the perfect place to holiday in summer or winter, but especially the latter. He also shared his intention to return soon and a humorous fishing story from his visit.

After promising to put his new rod and reel to use at the first opportunity, he exclaimed, "This has been the most enjoyable vacation I've had in a long time!"

At the end of the speeches, senior queen of the Galveston Oleander Festival, Kalia Humphreys, presented Roosevelt with an oil painting of oleanders by Emma Richardson Cherry, noted flower artist of Houston. Along with the painting came an announcement by the executive chairman of the festival, George Sealy, that the blooms at the center of the painting represented the new President Roosevelt variety of oleanders, named in honor of the visitor. This unique variety featured single blossoms of salmon-colored, whirling petals and yellow throats. Roosevelt proudly told the crowd that he planned to hang the painting in the White House as soon as he arrived.

The Washington group, now including Johnson, boarded the presidential train after the ceremony and left for Fort Worth.

With the departure of the White House staff, the Hotel Galvez relinquished its temporary designation and resumed its exclusive role as a luxury hotel.

President Franklin Delano Roosevelt in front of the Texas Heroes Monument on Broadway.

The day after Roosevelt left Galveston Island, George VI and Elizabeth were coronated as king and queen of the United Kingdom, and the White House sent a congratulatory letter to them that had been composed at the Hotel Galvez.

18

THE MOODY YEARS

In September 1940, William Lewis Moody Jr. purchased Hotel Galvez as an affiliate of the National Hotel Company. Founded in 1927, the corporation built such properties as Galveston's Buccaneer and Jean Lafitte hotels and purchased others, including the Menger in San Antonio, Mountain Lake in Virginia and the Hotel Washington in Washington, D.C. During the next three decades, the group would spend more than $1 million renovating, refurbishing and reinventing the Galvez. A priority was providing a private bathroom for each guest room, which reduced the number of total rooms but increased their appeal.

The Hotel Galvez participated in a scrap-metal drive for the prewar effort in July 1941, contributing old aluminum ware such as kitchen utensils, banquet rings, a waffle grill, a soup kettle, shower rings, malted milk shakers and other items the hotel no longer used. This, of course, would also make way for more desirable replacements.

Hotel Galvez was commandeered by the U.S. Coast Guard to be used as a barracks in 1942 and was temporarily closed to the general public. When the property was released back to the owners in 1944, a swift refurbishment took place, and the Galvez was once again able to accept tourists.

In the latter 1940s and 1950s, owners of the hotel indirectly profited, as it was a place to find accommodations near entertainment and illegal gambling that took place at the Balinese Room and other pier attractions. This influx of funds allowed the owners to bring the Galvez up to date.

Left: W.L. Moody and Mary Northen Moody beneath a banner on Hotel Galvez welcoming General Douglas MacArthur, 1951. *Courtesy of the Moody Family Archives.*

Below: Split seawall entrance to Twenty-First Street Pier in 1947. The entrance on the right led to Dreamland Café, that on the left to the Balinese Room. *Author's collection.*

177—Aerial View of Galveston from the Gulf of Mexico, Galveston, Texas

PHOTO COURTESY CHAMBER OF COMMERCE

7B-H168

The first Galveston Pleasure Pier, built in 1943, was geared to serve as a recreational facility for members of the military stationed in Galveston, who were forbidden from taking part in the action of the more popular casinos off the seawall. It quickly became the largest of its kind in the country, offering fishing facilities, a full carnival midway, an immense ballroom with live bands, an aquarium, an open-air stadium and an outdoor movie theater where patrons could enjoy the latest films under the stars.

As the hotel changed hands and incorporated updated decoration schemes through the years, some of the attempted additions were short-lived; others evolved. Descriptions of these rooms can sometimes seem humorous to modern sensibilities, though they were fashionable in their day.

Seeing the need for an exclusive entertainment option for the local social elite, the private Galvez Club opened its doors in July 1950. The initial membership fee for the club rooms was $300, with monthly dues of $6. The sign-up roster reached one hundred members by opening day.

Architect Tom M. Price transformed the former Terrace Room into a brightly colored Hawaiian theme lounge. Members had access to the private, air-conditioned lounge carpeted in a bold pattern featuring

Galveston Pleasure Pier with Murdoch's and Hotel Galvez in the background, 1951. *Author's collection.*

Left to right: Mrs. John W. Mecom, Carnes Weaver, Mrs. Weaver and Mr. Mecom in the Hawaiian Lounge at the Galvez Club. *Courtesy of Moody Family Archives.*

flowers native to Hawaii. Blond wood coffee tables and occasional tables and wood-paneled walls offered punctuation for the frenzy of colors in the rest of the appointments.

Beneath the tangerine-painted ceiling, guests relaxed in overstuffed mohair sectional divans of aqua blue, tangerine, brown and fuchsia. Block-printed, mohair drapes of chartreuse with fuchsia and brown accents adorned the windows, and island-appropriate potted tropical plants were stationed throughout the room. Diners could also take advantage of the open-air terrace overlooking the pool while sitting on canary yellow and royal blue cushions of the Philippine rattan table and chair sets.

Though the club rooms were open only to members, the heated swimming pool was also available to guests of the Galvez. Surrounded by a flagstone walkway, the thirty-by-seventy-five-foot pool featured lighting that allowed swimmers to enjoy the water at night, and an innovative system completely changed the water every eight hours.

Colorful lounge chairs upholstered in printed, waterproof sailcloth sat beneath large umbrellas on the pavement, allowing momentary escape from the Texas sun. Seventeen multicolored cabanas with striped awning curtains were positioned on two sides of the pool and furnished with chairs and tiled-

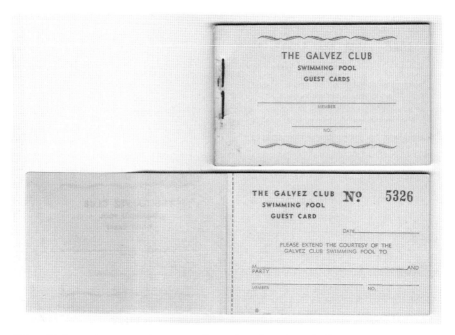

Galvez Club members were given passes for pool use in order to invite guests. *Courtesy of the Moody Family Archives.*

top tables to offer semiprivate dining spaces for diners ordering hamburgers and sodas from the grill.

The hotel's exterior was repainted white with green trim in 1954.

The success of the Galvez Club spurred management to expand affordable options to the tourist population, and in late June 1954, the ultramodern Galvez Villa motel addition opened for business. Surrounding the north and east sides of the swimming pool in an *L* shape, the villas were constructed on property formerly occupied by the Galveston Artillery Club.

Designed to mimic the Surf Rider Hotel of Honolulu, the Galvez Villa's fifty-one studio rooms and deluxe suites featured private, curving lanai balconies with roofs painted in alternating lime and raspberry. Each gray-green painted balcony had two aluminum armchairs, a lounge chair and a table. Guests could look out to the Gulf of Mexico, sunbath or relax with a cocktail.

Every room had a twenty-one-inch television, a seven-channel wall radio and individual controls for air conditioners. The warm yellow-walled guest rooms were arranged to accommodate entertaining. Two chairs upholstered in coral or golf green gros point mohair and two sofas provided comfortable seating for fifteen people around a Formica-topped coffee table.

Galvez Hotel and Villa, 1970s. *Author's collection.*

Galvez Villa pool and lanais, 1970s.

Hotel Galvez matchbook cover, circa 1950. *Author's collection.*

The desert sand–color dresser and desk combination with contracting walnut Formica top could double as a bar service area. Desk and floor lamps sported pale coral shades, and the floor was covered with a soft, green-flecked carpet. Drapes in a modernistic print of white background flecked with gold and symmetrical designs of deep forest green laced with lines of black and aqua blue could be pulled to cover the sliding glass door to the lanai for privacy. Watercolor scenes of Bermuda by artist Adolph Triner hung on the walls in frames of unfinished, knotted wood.

Suites designed to be shared by two couples could be divided with a draw drape partition. On one side, the living room provided foam rubber sofas that folded out into double beds; the other side offered a bedroom with twin beds. Family suites featured an alcove with two light wood bunk beds for the children.

Businesses proudly took out advertisements in the local paper to announce their involvement in the latest addition to the Hotel Galvez. Black Hardware Company provided plumbing fixtures; glass block and brickwork was done by contractor James A. Manning; lumber was supplied by Gulf Lumber Company and Waples Lumber; W.A. Kelso Building Material supplied the concrete and brick; Butterowe Sheet Metal Works roofed the addition; electrical installations were done by Britain Electric Company; and Milton Pate was the project's paint contractor.

Pride of participation aside, the Villa was less than popular with local purists, who were dismayed at the bawdy addition to the historic hotel.

Oleanders and hibiscus lined the south wall of the addition, and bougainvillea vines were planted along a cyclone fence in the rear to incorporate the tropical theme.

The Galvez Villa was promoted with colorful brochures and newspaper ads that emphasized a fun, Hawaiian feel.

Hotel Galvez and Villa, 1950s.

Water damage to the ground floor of the main hotel during Hurricane Carla in 1961 offered the opportunity to make minor updates to the hotel while making repairs.

Management of the Hotel Galvez proudly opened a new "Garden Wing" in the east wing of the sixth floor of the main hotel on February 4, 1962. It included a hospitality suite named the Galvez Garden that was available for conventions, conferences and private parties.

White painted wrought-iron panels mounted flat against the wall surrounded the doorway to the Garden Wing, with a carriage lamp and a slender tree at each side. Guests passed through saloon-style wood swinging doors to enter. Once inside, a garden-and-patio setting surrounded visitors. Stone wall patterned wallpaper gave the impression of an enclosed garden, and windows were framed with green outdoor shutters.

Potted plants and a large potted orange tree bearing fruit were positioned around the room, and a continuous waterfall feature and small fountains completed the design. Carriage lamps provided lighting for the space and could be dimmed for a twilight effect. The focal point of the suite was an oval, mahogany-paneled bar surrounded by high metal stools upholstered in green, gold and shell pink fabrics.

Sales manager John H. Hughes proudly told visiting press that the decor of the Garden Wing was created by Thelma S. Reaney, the hotel's executive housekeeper.

The hall featured a flagstone path floor, and a canopy of pale green and yellow awning covered the ceiling.

The unique hospitality area shared the Garden Wing with seven bedrooms and one two-room suite. The doors of the guest rooms were painted in pastel colors, and the name of a flowering tree or shrub was written on each. Rich textiles in rainbow hues decorated the interiors of these guest rooms to complete the nod to fanciful gardens.

The hotel management was pleased that the Garden Suite was completed in time for the first large convention of the year, during which over four hundred delegates and their guests visited the whimsical rooms.

The hotel's Galvez Club received a "face lift" at the same time, incorporating designs by Bernard Spitzr, an interior decorator with Plantowsky's. Its trademark Mexican tile floor was covered with wall-to-wall tweed carpet in soft blues and greens, and Spanish patterned blue-and-green draperies were hung from the windows. Contemporary walnut chairs and tables and new, low-hanging light fixtures suspended from brass chains were added.

Just three years later, the club sported yet another decor, an African motif, and was renamed the Safari Room, with zebra skins, tribal masks and hunting trophies hung on the walls.

Galvestonians enjoyed events at the Galvez Club through all the changes, attending South of the Border parties, spring fashion show luncheons, New Year's Eve parties, bingo dinners, coffee and ice cream socials, Western-style barbecues, luaus, floor shows, St. Patrick's Day parties and dinner dances.

The one taste that remained fairly constant at the Galvez Club was Bloody Marys. The hotel's version had the reputation of being the best on the island, mixed up by bartender Jack Cleveland in the 1970s.

Beginning in July 1965, a two-year, $1 million renovation took place. The exterior of Hotel Galvez was resurfaced and the interior completely refurbished, resulting in 260 guest rooms and 7 meeting rooms. Brilliant red carpeting was installed in rooms and hallways, televisions were installed in every room, deluxe apartments were arranged on the top floor and, most important, the entire building was air-conditioned. Only certain areas of the hotel had previously provided this luxury. The kitchen was completely refitted with stainless-steel counters and red-tile floors, and the main ballroom was repainted Wedgewood blue with pale blue ceilings trimmed in Swedish red.

Cover of 1958 luau invitation to Galvez Club members. *Courtesy of Moody Family Archives.*

View of Hotel Galvez and Villa from Gulf, circa 1975. *Author's collection.*

Permanent guests, or those who lived at the hotel year-round, had full access to its amenities. Families were allowed to store items in the attic and keep children's bikes in the basement. Adults could amuse themselves with a game of shuffleboard by the pool or practice their skills on an Astroturf putting green. A Teen Room with Ping-Pong tables and a jukebox downstairs became a popular gathering place for younger residents and guests.

As the end of the 1960s approached, profits at the hotel declined, and in 1971, the Galvez was sold to department store owner Harvey McCarty of Rock Island, Illinois, and local retired physician Leon Bromberg.

In 1973, McCarty held an open house to show updated rooms and instituted year-round winter rates to encourage bookings. The cost of rooms ranged from $13.50 to $19.50 for one person, $17.50 to $22.50 for two and suites starting at $25.00.

He also changed the name of Galvez Hotel and Villa to Galvez Hotel and Motel, feeling the word *villa* did not properly reflect Galveston.

In his first two years of ownership, bookings increased by 25 percent.

19

COAST GUARD YEARS

The U.S. Coast Guard did not officially utilize the hotel as a living and working facility until the last civilian guest moved out in 1942. Those who lived at the hotel year-round, referred to as "permanent guests," were given time to find other living quarters.

In the meantime, social functions and meetings of public groups at the hotel came to an end. Hotel manager Jimmie R. Gray stated that the weekly meeting of the Rotary Club, which had held its luncheons there since 1913, would be the last civilian event for the duration of the war.

Though the coast guard had not yet moved into the Hotel Galvez, signs were posted at all of the entrances on September 9, 1942, notifying the public that the property was under control of the United States Coast Guard and was therefore no longer open to the public. By the end of October, the Galvez had been completely transformed from a resort hotel into a military barracks. The 250-room hotel housed as many as one thousand coastguardsmen at times.

Even the once-lavish bridal suites were outfitted with multiple bunk beds to provide accommodations for the new residents. A wardroom was established in the ladies' parlor, providing an area for discussions of a much different nature than had been held by the genteel guests who previously occupied the room.

A bugler would sound the call as coastguardsmen filed down the marble stairs for mealtime in the mess, and a large ship's bell was installed in a frame on the lawn and rung on the hours and half hours between six in the morning and nine at night, just as would be heard aboard a U.S. Coast Guard ship.

A third-class post office was opened at the hotel, where two mail specialist coastguardsmen were responsible for canceling and sending outgoing mail and sorting incoming letters. One of these specialists was Gray, the former manager of Hotel Galvez before the coast guard took over the property. He was soon promoted to lieutenant and put in charge of the Officers' Quarters at the hotel.

The United States Coast Guard Auxiliary, the volunteer uniformed auxiliary service of the coast guard, met for regular classes at the Hotel Galvez. Guest speakers and instructors would share with the men their knowledge of judo, diesel-engine construction and maintenance, semaphore and flag signals and patrol tactics.

Thanksgiving of that year brought a dinner reminiscent of the Galvez's dining fare. The servicemen were treated to roast turkey and dressing and cranberry sauce and fruitcake. Illustrated menus printed on the basement

Members of the U.S. Coast Guard relaxing outside their Hotel Galvez barracks during World War II.

press were placed on each table to serve as mementoes of the special meal. That evening, for the first time since the hotel became a barracks, a number of civilians were again able to enjoy dancing in the Galvez ballroom as guests of the coast guard. Besides the local married couples who were able to obtain invitations at the barracks, single women (much to the delight of the 1,500 servicemen present) were also allowed to attend.

Females who were members of the MSO (Maritime Security Operations), GSO (Girls' Service Organization) or Minute Girls (a patriotic emergency service order of Camp Fire Girls) had clearance from their work at the Galveston chapter of the USO (United Service Organization) to attend. Any girls who were not members of those organizations could only be present as a date of a coastguardsman and after registering with the Servicemen's Bureau before the day of the event.

All of the unmarried women attending were given instructions about the "dos" and "don'ts" of interacting with the servicemen. Leaving the dance with a gentleman was not allowed. Most of the attendees were thrilled just to have dance partners with whom to enjoy the music of Bill Cantrell and his orchestra as a distraction from daily responsibilities. It was the first of several such dances held at the Galvez.

The officers of the U.S. Coast Guard made time for celebrations as well and held an early New Year's Eve dance for officers, their wives and friends at the barracks on December 30 to welcome the coming of 1943. Invitations were extended to men of the naval section base, port director's office, marine hospital, Port Arthur and Houston coastguardsmen and Hitchcock Naval Air Station. Guests arrived at 9:00 p.m. and were treated to music provided by the Coast Guard Orchestra, a floorshow and refreshments.

Besides the daily obligations of coast guard duties, the men who lived at the hotel assisted during community emergencies. A bolt of lightning struck a cotton warehouse and set it ablaze in May 1943. For over six hours, a force of 350 coastguardsmen, city firemen, auxiliary firemen and cotton company employees fought the fire. The local newspaper reported that 200 coastguardsmen, including 40 from the regular coast guard fire brigade, were on hand at the fire, many having been called out from the barracks at the Galvez. They aided firemen in handling water lines, pulling hoses as they climbed atop burning bales of cotton to pour water onto them.

At least ten city firemen and coastguardsmen received treatment at John Sealy Hospital and the sick bay at the coast guard barracks for severely reddened eyes. Nearly all of the men who fought the blaze suffered reddened eyes to some degree. Miraculously, there were no life-threatening injuries.

Quarterly "Church by the Sea" services were held at the barracks, officiated by Chaplain William McNeill of the army air base. The Coast Guard Choir provided music, and guest choirs such as the one from the First Presbyterian Church sang additional songs. Held in the evening at 7:30 p.m., these services were open to the public, who, to maintain security, was asked to use only the west entrance to the Galvez.

In their spare time, the men participated in a wide range of activities, such as playing music in the Coast Guard Quartet and the Coast Guard Orchestra, singing in the Coast Guard Choir, riding bicycles along the seawall, playing baseball in the Service Baseball League and holding boxing matches in a ring set up on the lawn.

The men stationed at the Galvez received a special surprise in September 1943, when Jack Dempsey, who had reigned as the world heavyweight boxing champion from 1919 to 1926, stopped at the barracks for a visit. The sports hero was also a lieutenant commander in the coast guard stationed in Manhattan Beach, New York, and was in Galveston on leave. After finishing lunch on a Sunday afternoon with friends at a local café, where he was mobbed by fans, Dempsey decided that it would be appropriate to attend the opening game of the Service League playoffs between the coast guard and Camp Wallace. When he arrived at the field, the players insisted that he throw out the first ball.

After the game, Dempsey went to the Hotel Galvez to speak to the men who lived at the barracks. Standing in the boxing ring, he told the gathering that there was a parallel between fighting in the ring and fighting during wartime. "Once you get an opponent backing up, don't ease up. Give 'em hell. When you've got them on the run, keep them on the run," advised the heavyweight champion.

That evening, he left the barracks for Houston, where he was scheduled to referee fights in a war-bond show a few hours later. The excitement of meeting such a popular athlete was undoubtedly the highlight of many of the men's time at the Hotel Galvez.

After functioning as a working facility for the U.S. Coast Guard for two years, the Hotel Galvez was relinquished in March 1944. Officials of the hotel chain shared high praise to Lieutenant Commander Walter G. Etheridge and his staff for the excellent care they had taken of the property during their occupation.

The Galvez was officially turned over to its owners, the Affiliated National Hotels, on June 30, and invitations were issued to a special military ceremony to be held on August 20, stating, "After two years of meritorious service to the

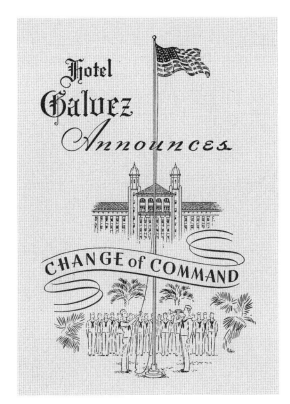

Left: Invitation to the official Change of Command celebration, ending the hotel's service as a U.S. Coast Guard barracks, 1944.

Below: Interior of Change of Command celebration invitation.

★ ★TEXAS' FINEST SEASIDE RESORT HOTEL ★
Announces CHANGE of COMMAND ★ ★ ★ ★ ★ ★

On August 20th the South's finest seaside resort, Hotel Galvez, after two years of meritorious service, will be given an honorable discharge by the United States Coast Guard and returned to civilian use.

In announcing the change of command (returning to civilian use) of this magnificent hotel, the owners have spared no efforts to restore the Galvez. In its new luxurious appointments, it again assumes the position of the most modern and beautiful rendezvous on the Gulf.

A cordial invitation is extended to all former patrons and new comers to Galveston to visit the Hotel Galvez, a vacation spot known to all the Southwest.

Loyd Bumpas, *Manager*

Hotel Galvez
GALVESTON, TEXAS

★ ★ ★ ★ ★

United States Coast Guard, the Hotel Galvez has been given an honorable discharge, to be returned to civilian use."

To meet the desire to reopen the Galvez to the public as soon as possible, work began immediately to restaff and update the hotel, including adding luxury apartments. Loyd Bumpass of Omaha, Nebraska, was hired to serve as the new manager. He and his wife, Elizabeth, brought their family to Galveston and immediately began tending to the details of the project.

Workmen and artisans began working on the floors as the coast guard vacated them, replacing carpet, painting walls and installing new furniture.

Bumpass hired a new staff for the hotel and began training personnel to ensure the transition from government property back into luxury accommodations went smoothly.

With so much to be accomplished, the decision was made to open sections of the hotel as they were completed to meet the numerous requests of hopeful guests.

Chef Coleman was hired to oversee the Hotel Galvez Coffee Shop, which had been thoroughly renovated with modern kitchen equipment and decor in the dining area. Coleman had extensive catering experience in this country and abroad, having worked at the Cecil Hotel in London, the Montmartre in France and such well-known American hotels and restaurants as Rectors in New York, Dutros famous seafood house in Minneapolis and the Blackstone in Chicago. He came to Galveston from another Affiliated Hotel property, the Hotel Faust in Rockford, Illinois.

The new coffee shop manager, Marjorie Watkins, formerly of Schrafft's New York and Hotel Washington in Washington, D.C., opened the doors to the public on August 13.

Ten days later, Bumpass extended invitations to the community to attend the long-awaited reopening of the Hotel Galvez.

Guest rooms soon filled with vacationers as well as naval and military personnel and other war workers on travel duty, and the Hotel Galvez was poised to resume its place as one of the most popular resort destinations in the Southwest.

20

SECRET STORM OF 1943

An unlikely string of circumstances during the summer of 1943 resulted in the citizens of Galveston being taken off guard by a major hurricane.

During World War II, German navy U-boats (short for *Unterseeboot*, the German word for submarine) prowled the Gulf of Mexico, including Galveston's coastline. This threat resulted in silencing radio reports from ships at sea to prevent the Nazis from determining their positions. Unfortunately, those offshore communications normally provided the weather bureau with information crucial to receiving data about coming weather threats in order to issue adequate storm warnings to civilians. Once any weather advisories were developed, they also required clearance via communications, also impeded, with the New Orleans bureau office before they could be released to the public.

Due to incomplete weather updates, Galvestonians went about their business unaware of the coming hurricane as late as Monday, the day before the hurricane struck. Just after lunch hour on July 27, the powerful storm hit the island and continued through the evening, quite literally blowing the storm's secret cover.

Coastguardsmen stationed at the Hotel Galvez and surrounding areas were alerted and made preparations to aid their host city.

A storm-warning switchboard staffed by the chamber of commerce fielded hundreds of calls for information, attempting to answer as many as possible. The unnamed hurricane soon ended their efforts, breaking a skylight and tearing off part of the roof of their building. Shortly after 11:00 p.m., a coast guard truck arrived to take the marooned chamber workers to their homes.

Port Bolivar residents trapped in their homes were also evacuated by coast guard ships and trucks and brought to Galveston for shelter.

Eyewitnesses later shared stories about how the coastguardsmen bravely risked personal injury, battling high winds and torrential rain to patrol the streets during the storm and remove approximately one hundred people from dangerous locations to the safety of their barracks at the Hotel Galvez. Physicians and their assistants waited at the hotel to provide medical attention if needed.

The servicemen who remained at the Galvez shared coats and blankets with the storm refugees and served coffee throughout the day.

Rough seas forced the United States Army dredge *Galveston* inside the jetties of the harbor. Winds reaching hurricane velocity caused the dredge to drag its anchor by noon, and despite valiant efforts by its captain and crew, the *Galveston* struck the rocks at 2:50 p.m. and sank. As the ship began to disintegrate, the older and physically disabled members of the crew set off to the jetty in the only intact lifeboat, and the rest of the men abandoned ship on orders from the captain.

Because of the interrupted telephone service, the coast guard did not learn of the wreck until 8:30 p.m. Rescue operations were postponed until daybreak due to hazardous conditions.

In the first attempt to rescue the stranded dredge crew, a thirty-six-foot coast guard launch was put out of control when the motor failed.

Early on the morning of July 28, a coast guard boat commanded by Commander Walter Etheridge fought its way through Bolivar Roads to rescue the marooned men. After two attempts to reach the site while battling fierce waves, the men who had clung to the rock jetty throughout the night were successfully rescued. Others were cast adrift and managed to reach the Bolivar shore. One man was found clinging to the dredge's smokestack above the water line, and another washed ashore alive on Thursday afternoon.

The rescued men were taken to Pier 18, where ambulances waited to carry them to the Marina Hospital. In all, the coast guard rescued forty-eight men, thirty-nine of whom were injured. Of the *Galveston* crew, eleven lost their lives. Captain Lane, who could not swim, went down with his ship.

Two coast guard launches continued to search for survivors as they gathered the bodies of the victims that were scattered along ten miles of the beach.

The tug *Titan* also foundered at sea, and the guard found a few of its lucky survivors, whose life rafts had washed ashore on Bolivar Beach.

Though a handful of stories about the storm appeared in the local paper, reports detailing damage from the storm were highly censored to prevent enemy forces from ascertaining the loss of war materials. The Federal Bureau of Investigation reportedly closed a La Porte telegraph office after a telegram containing information about the damage was sent. To this day, the local weather office has no official information about the storm, any reports and data having been classified and sent to Washington.

Of the few tales that survived were those of the heroism of the men of the coast guard and how kind they were to refugees seeking their help on land and sea. It was one of the many times throughout the history of the Galvez when the community found safety and relief in its halls.

21

CELEBRITIES

Numerous well-known politicians, military men, movie stars and other entertainers stayed at the Hotel Galvez when they visited or performed on the island. Imagine checking in to the hotel and seeing Groucho Marx or Frank Sinatra strolling toward the elevators.

Beginning during Prohibition, Galveston Island earned the nickname the "Free State of Galveston" due to its freewheeling reputation of gambling, bootlegging and other not-so-secret illegal activities that continued into the 1930s and '40s. Galveston became the "Playground of the Southwest," outshining New Orleans a few hundred miles to the east.

The popular Balinese Room stood on a pier extending over the water just across from the Galvez. Owned by former Galvez barber Sam Maceo and his brother Rosario, the private supper club was most famous for its casino at the back. Local authorities at the time had a reputation of turning their heads when it came to illegal businesses that profited Galveston.

Maceo quickly developed a reputation for hiring only first-class entertainment for his clubs at the Balinese and the Hollywood Dinner Club. The combination of offerings, both legal and not, lured tourists and celebrities alike.

The casinos of Las Vegas didn't appear on the scene until the 1940s, making Galveston a unique entertainment destination. The future members of the famous Las Vegas Rat Pack of the 1960s all performed in Galveston long before their days on the Vegas Strip.

From left to right: Sam Maceo, pianist Carmen Caballero and Mayor Herbert Y. Cartwright at the Balinese Room, early 1950s.

Many celebrities who either performed or visited Maceo's Balinese Room or Hollywood Dinner Club visited or stayed at the Hotel Galvez, where Maceo himself lived with his family in a penthouse apartment. Guests included Joey Bishop, Guy Lombardo, Rudy Vallee, Fred Astaire, Jimmy Stewart, Peggy Lee, director and Galveston native King Vidor, Sammy Davis

Jr., Duke Ellington, Howard Hughes, Dean Martin, Jerry Lewis, Jack Benny, Edgar Bergen and Charlie McCarthy, Jack Dempsey, Jimmy Dorsey, Peter Lawford, Art Linkletter, Dorothy Lamour, Mel Torme, Jayne Mansfield, Tony Bennett, the Three Stooges, George Burns and Gracie Allen, Arthur Murray, Gene Autry and Bob Hope.

Bandleader Phil Harris often performed at Maceo's establishments and became so enamored of Galveston that he adopted it as his second home. One of his band members wrote the song "My Galveston Gal," which became quite popular, bringing even more national attention to the island.

Harris married movie star and G.I. pinup girl Alice Faye in Sam Maceo's penthouse apartment at the Hotel Galvez in September 1941, with Maceo serving as his best man.

Galveston's Badgett quadruplets were often special guests of the Galvez and made numerous appearances there. Celebrity sisters Joan, Joyce, Jeraldine and Jeanette were known as "Galveston's Sweethearts." They served as honorary flower girls for the Alice Faye/Phil Harris wedding, sold war bonds and posed with Johnny Weissmuller of the Tarzan movies during the 1946 Splash Days.

Bandleader Phil Harris and actress Alice Faye's wedding in Sam Maceo's penthouse apartment at the Hotel Galvez.

Alice Fay with Badgett quadruplets and wedding guests in the Maceo apartment at the Hotel Galvez.

Phil Harris with Badgett quadruplets flower girls at his wedding.

Solo transatlantic aviator Douglas "Wrong Way" Corrigan revisited his hometown in 1938. A celebratory dinner was held for him at the hotel after he was the honoree of a ticker-tape parade in town.

Several U.S. presidents and other dignitaries stayed at the Hotel Galvez as well. Though President Franklin Delano Roosevelt's core White House staff stayed in the Hotel Galvez in 1937, the president himself stayed aboard his ship offshore.

When the Hotel Galvez was commandeered as a barracks by the U.S. Coast Guard during World War II, the clubs were declared off-limits to the military men. Luckily, this interruption of the long mutually beneficial relationship with the Galvez and the Balinese did not end the flow of well-known personalities who chose to stay at the Galvez.

In 1949, war hero and future president General Dwight D. Eisenhower was honored at a reception held at Hotel Galvez. He and his wife, Mamie, held a brief press conference on their arrival at the hotel. Photographs were taken and interviews held before the couple attended the luncheon at the Galvez. They stayed in the Presidential Suite, which was redecorated especially for the occasion before their arrival.

During the annual convention of the Texas Press Association held at the Galvez in 1955, Vice President Richard Nixon gave a scheduled address and then spent the night at the hotel. Secret Service men arrived ahead

Buccaneer Hotel, Murdoch's and Hotel Galvez on the seawall, 1951.

of his visit to conduct background and security checks on hotel personnel. A popular political figure at the time, locals were eager to catch a glimpse of Nixon during his visit. One local official commented the he was "more handsome than most movie stars."

U.S. senator and future president Lyndon Baines Johnson and his wife, Ladybird, stayed at the hotel in 1959. In 1968, Hubert Humphrey held a press conference at Hotel Galvez during his unsuccessful bid for the presidency.

General Douglas MacArthur and Texas governor William P. Hobby also signed the hotel register during visits to the island.

HURRICANE CARLA

One of the strongest storms of the century struck the Texas coast on Monday, September 11, 1961, the same year John F. Kennedy was inaugurated as the thirty-fifth president of the United States. Hurricane Carla was the most intense storm the island had experienced since 1900. It battered Galveston from Sunday, September 10, until the early morning hours of Tuesday, September 12.

Many Galveston residents heeded precautionary general evacuation warnings that began on Friday, using the new seventy-two-foot-high causeway that had opened earlier that year to cross to the mainland. By the following day, tides were already five to six feet above normal. Once the ferries ceased to run due to tides and winds on the leading edge of the storm, the causeway was the only way to reach the mainland. Only one lane of the roadway remained open by midmorning on Sunday, and it was used to travel in both directions, causing a serious risk to travelers.

When the causeway closed at 11:00 a.m., forty thousand to fifty thousand people on the island who had not evacuated had no other option than to find shelter. The hotels and motels quickly filled to capacity, with many families choosing to shelter at the Galvez.

Even with the large number of people entering its doors, the Galvez's staff saw to guests' comfort, placing an enormous bowl of fresh fruit in the lobby.

Although it had been forbidden, some people succeeded in sneaking their pets into the Galvez. Once there, the animals were not turned away from shelter.

Hotel Galvez with original red façade, circa 1960. *Courtesy of Moody Family Archive.*

Dedicated workers from the *Galveston Daily News* wrapped the morning papers to keep them dry and waded through water to deliver them to the Hotel Galvez. The newspaper missed printing just one issue, due to the presses not having electricity to run.

Winds and rain began to batter Galveston on Sunday, and people inside the Galvez watched through the windows as a transformer pole rocked back and forth in the fury of the storm. A power company crew arrived and attached it to their truck with a long guy wire in an attempt to stabilize it, but the pole eventually broke free and fell.

By Sunday afternoon, the power had failed and there was no running water above the second floor. The guests were asked to come to the lobby for pitchers of water, as the staff was too taxed to bring them to the rooms.

On the first floor, wind forced through storm shutters created a high-pitched sound that was compared to factory whistles.

The hotel had a large supply of flashlights and lanterns for the staff and guests, and everyone made an attempt to reserve their batteries.

Carla barreled toward the shore as a category 5 hurricane, weakening to a strong category 4 storm just before making landfall on Monday.

One of the floor-to-ceiling glass windows in the Grecian Room crashed in, and others were shattered by flying debris. Eventually, the staff gave up on mopping the water that continually seeped onto the lobby floor.

KGBC, one of Galveston's two radio stations, was able to remain on the air throughout the storm to air weather reports and news about what was going on around the city. People in rooms of the Galvez gathered around shared radios to listen to the reports. Though telephone lines never went down, local amateur radio operators supplied most of the communication across the island.

Meals at the Galvez were served military-style in the enclosed dining room to guests who sometimes stood in ankle-deep water to retrieve food for their families. Hot coffee was served around the clock, just as it had been during the storm of 1915.

People shared reading materials they had brought with them, trying to distract themselves and their families from the storm outside. Many guests eventually retreated to their rooms to get some sleep, exhausted from the storm-watching vigil.

Off Galveston Island, people around the nation were able to watch the progress of the storm on their televisions.

A little-known reporter from KHOU-TV in Houston devised a unique way to communicate the size and danger of the storm to his audience, forever changing the way weather was reported to the public. Dan Rather stood in the lobby of Hotel Galvez witnessing rooms filled with people who could no longer get a room. He was soon reporting live atop the seawall about the coming hurricane.

He and his crew set up inside the local weather station ahead of the storm and were able to report directly from the second floor of the building when Carla struck just south of Galveston. Other news outlets had been sealed off from reporting on the island when the causeway closed.

It was the first live television broadcast during a hurricane.

The native Texan was also the first to broadcast a radar image of a hurricane and its eye on television, creating a visual reference to convince the public of imminent danger.

Handing a meteorologist a piece of transparent plastic, Rather asked him to draw a scaled outline of the Texas coast to put the image on the radar into perspective. Viewers were shocked to see that the storm was the size of the Gulf of Mexico. CBS News in New York broadcast Rather's live coverage, and the recognition landed him the position of national correspondent.

At 3:15 a.m. on Tuesday morning, the first of two tornadoes spawned by the hurricane hit Galveston, breaking windows on the inland side of the hotel. Thought to be one of the most intense tornadoes to ever strike Galveston, the F4 killed eight people and destroyed over sixty buildings.

The nearby wood Mountain Speedway roller coaster was blown apart by the storm. Amusement rides and vendor stands on the Pleasure Pier took the brunt force of tornadic winds, which devastated the iconic tourist attraction. The steel diving tower used for diving exhibitions on the pier was twisted and unceremoniously dropped into the water.

Though everything on top of the pier was destroyed, the pier itself held strong. Four years later, the Flagship Hotel opened atop the concrete platform. Damage inflicted on the Flagship during Hurricane Ike in 2008 unfortunately closed the hotel, leading to the birth of the present Pleasure Pier.

During the height of the 1961 storm, an enormous whale, whose skeleton is still displayed at the Houston Museum of Natural Science, washed ashore, bearing witness to the strength of Carla.

Thankfully, the Hotel Galvez came through the event with relatively minimal damage. Part of the roofing had blown off, many windows were blown out and the carpeting was ruined when water came in the ground floor.

But everyone inside was safe and knew once again that their Queen of the Gulf had taken care of its people. Guests who stayed in rooms at the Galvez for the full three days were charged $9.50 per night plus tax, a total of $29.97 for three nights of protection and care.

23

GALVEZ RADIO

Having a radio station share space with a luxury hotel certainly isn't an everyday occurrence, but it worked to the advantage of both in the mid-1970s.

On September 2, 1957, a group of Galveston businessmen purchased KLUF radio from Mayor George Roy Clough (pronounced just like the radio acronym) and promptly changed the call letters to KILE, beginning a rocking new era of music on the island.

The call letters were meant to be a play on the word "isle," and the logo featured a palm tree in place of the letter *i*.

Purchasing all-new equipment, the new owners launched a fresh Top 40, rock and roll format previously unheard of across Galveston airwaves. Those were the days of Elvis, Chuck Berry and the Everly Brothers.

Mornings started with a lively show called *Hit the Deck*, and afternoons were filled with the latest releases during *Teen Tempos*.

The owners soon moved their popular new station from a small building on Broadway to a newly outfitted studio and office in the basement of the Hotel Galvez, right across the street from the beach where many of their listeners spent most of their free time.

The station operated with a typically laid-back Galveston friendliness. Teenagers who were cruising along the seawall could pull up to the Galvez, walk into the radio station and personally make requests to the DJ.

In 1969, it would have been one of the first stations to play Glen Campbell's famous hit song "Galveston."

Front façade of Hotel Galvez, 1968.

KILE's clever team kept Galvestonians on their toes with promotional stunts that were wildly unexpected and entertaining at the time, from playing a certain newly released song for twenty-four hours straight to a personal appearance by an elephant.

The Lone Star Buggy Beach Report vehicle bounced along the sand, conducting live interviews with visitors along the seawall.

On Saturdays, sunbathers listening to KILE on transistor radios would hear the reminder "Turn before you burn" played every half hour, reminding them to roll over on their beach towels at the beach or poolside.

The radio station and its employees regularly participated in fundraising for the March of Dimes and participating in Muscular Dystrophy Telethons, food drives and other causes.

It originated the long-running Battle of the Bands event held at Menard Park during Galveston's Shrimp Festival, awarding a trophy that stood over six feet tall to the winner.

One of the most popular and long-running shows on KILE during its Galvez days was a Sunday night show called *For Lovers Only*, during which disc jockey Dave Martin would play songs about love. Listeners could call or write in, requesting songs to be dedicated to their sweethearts, and local teens would listen eagerly in hopes of hearing that some secret schoolmate had dedicated a special song for them.

Among the sometimes rambunctious radio crew in the basement of a luxury hotel were Vandy Anderson, Rusty Draper, Dave Martin, Darrell

Invitation to Galveston
Artillery Club Ball, 1968.

Hendrix, Mark Russell, Tom Tyler, Kenny Miles, Pam Ivey, John Walton, Dean Daily, Bob Ford, Lou Muller, Steve Canyon, Ray Flores, Larry Sanville, Chris Allen, Moss Thornton, Joe Halstead, Rex Russell and many others, all popular with locals and visitors.

The radio station later located to a building on Avenue Q before being sold in April 1985. It was the end of an era for music-loving beachgoers.

24

MARRIOTT HOTELS

When Harvey McCarty and Leon Bromberg listed the Galvez for sale, the seaside hotel acquired a local celebrity as one of its new owners.

Renowned Houston heart surgeon Dr. Denton Cooley and Archie Bennett Jr. formed Mariner-Galvez, Limited, with an equal partnership in order to purchase and renovate the landmark hotel. The deal was brokered through Cooley's son-in-law, Houston realtor Constantin Kladis, in late August 1978.

Though the new owners attempted to remain anonymous during the acquisition process, it is almost impossible to keep secrets on a small island. Galveston was thrilled that the famous Texas doctor had arrived to breathe new life into its beloved hotel.

The property would be renamed the Galvez Marriott and managed by Mariner Corporation under a franchise agreement with the Marriott hotel chain.

On November 1, the last sixteen tenants of the hotel were asked to vacate the premises by December 8 so that work could begin. After the project was complete, the Galvez would no longer house permanent residents, due to Marriott regulations.

For one of the few times in its history, the hotel completely closed its doors to accommodate the massive undertaking.

During the renovations, the Hotel Galvez was added to the National Register of Historic Places in 1979; the following year, it was designated as a Texas Historic Landmark by the Texas Historical Commission.

Workmen preparing grounds for the 1980 reopening of Hotel Galvez. *Author's collection.*

John Kirksey Associates of Houston conducted an extensive survey of the property and concluded that nothing of architectural significance above the first floor had survived previous renovations. There was no congruity among the upper-floor guest rooms that had been reconfigured three to four times during past ownerships, and no original details were thought to remain.

An estimated $10 million endeavor began with completely gutting the interior from the second floor up, removing existing structures down to the exterior walls, columns, stairs and elevators. The massive 11-room penthouse on the seventh floor was subdivided into 4 separate guest rooms. The other 223 rooms on the second through sixth floors would all be designed with a standard format, furnishings and decor. Jeffrey Howard and Associates of Coral Gables, Florida, was hired to design the updated interiors.

On the first floor, false walls and ceilings that had been added during previous remodels were removed, revealing original wood ceilings, French doors, windows and open spaces that allowed sunlight to flow into the rooms once again. A crew of skilled craftsmen replaced damaged moldings and cornices, and the hotel's original chandeliers were refurbished and reinstalled.

The stucco façade was cleaned, repaired and painted white, and the red-tile roof was refurbished. Plans dictated that the entrance be relocated to the north side porte cochere, its original position.

One of the most dramatic changes to the exterior was created when the southern entrance was enclosed to facilitate an indoor-outdoor pool area directly off the lobby.

The two-story Villa motel addition and its pool were demolished, a change welcomed by the community, to provide space for a parking lot on the east side of the hotel.

Frank O'Keefe, who was previously the executive president of the Grand Hotel Company in Mackinac, Michigan, accepted the position as manager of the newly redesigned hotel.

The original portrait of Bernardo de Gálvez that was hung in the hotel in 1911 was restored through the kindness of Mr. and Mrs. F. Russell Kendall of Houston and for a second time took its place in the Galvez, watching over guests.

By the time the Galvez Marriott hosted its reopening ceremony on June 10, 1980, renovations had exceeded the original estimates, reaching the $12 million mark.

Indoor swimming pool facing the seawall, circa 1980. *Author's collection.*

Hotel Galvez with indoor-outdoor swimming pool, circa 1980s.

At the reopening celebration, longtime Hotel chief engineer Robert Franklin Warren was asked to cut the ribbon with the same pair of scissors used in the first grand opening sixty-nine years earlier. Secretary of State George W. Strake Jr. presented a Texas state flag to fly over the hotel and Truett Lattimer, executive director of the Texas Historical Commission, officially presented the Texas Historical Landmark designation.

Room rates at the new Marriott property started at approximately $100 per night, but by 1983, the franchise would begin offering off-season discounts and coupons that could reduce the rates to almost half that amount.

August 1983 brought the small but powerful Hurricane Alicia to the Texas coast, and 350 people took shelter in the Galvez Marriott. As extreme winds and debris battered the building, oceanfront windows were shattered and tiles were blown from the roof. Torrential rains drove through the openings once covered with glass, and guests were evacuated to the basement. Interior walls on two floors collapsed, their sheetrock soaked with water blown through the broken windows. Extensive damage to the hotel interior included walls, windows, roof tiles, furnishings and carpet, and the Galvez was compelled to close until the following January to complete repairs.

Two years after celebrating the Galvez's seventy-fifth anniversary in 1986, owners of the Queen of the Gulf declared bankruptcy and put it

Stereoview photograph of the Hotel Galvez Sun Parlor, showing wicker rockers.

up for auction to repay the $7.68 million debt owed to the Aetna Life Insurance Company.

After the deaths of Dr. Cooley and his wife, Louise, the contents of their Cool Acres Ranch, once featured in *Architectural Digest*, were auctioned off in October 2019. Many of the furnishings of House Number 4 on the property were originally from the Hotel Galvez, including iconic white wicker furniture.

GEORGE P. AND CYNTHIA MITCHELL

G alveston Preservationists George P. and Cynthia Woods Mitchell purchased the historic Galvez from Aetna in 1993 for $3 million with a vision of returning the Queen of the Gulf to the southern charm it once represented.

The Mitchells were leaders in the restoration of historic properties along the city's Strand District and instrumental in creating the landmark district that now exists. The T. Jefferson League Building was one of more than twenty Galveston properties saved and restored by the couple.

At one point, Mitchell Properties owned eighteen buildings in the Strand District and Pier 21, as well as Hotel Galvez, the Tremont House and the Harbor House Hotel & Marina.

In the years preceding the Mitchells' ownership of Hotel Galvez, the grand old lady had suffered a visible decline. Cynthia Mitchell once said to her husband, "If you really care about Galveston, you'll buy the Galvez."

The San Antonio architectural firm Ford, Powell & Carson was hired, and a three-year, $20 million project to restore the interiors and landscape to their original 1911 appearances began.

One of the first priorities was to remove the indoor pool, which permeated the lobby and restaurant with an unpleasant chlorine smell. With the pool structure gone, plans went forward to return the circular drive, broad walkways and palm court to the seawall side of the Galvez.

Luckily, one of the original twenty-two-foot canary palms that were planted during the hotel's dedication ceremony in 1911 still exists on the

Coin from the 1997 Hotel Galvez
Mardi Gras. *Author's collection.*

grounds. Added to it were fifty-four Filifera palms, estimated to be forty to fifty years old, from Arizona, and fifty Washingtonia and Sabal palms.

A new outdoor pool with a swim-up bar, heated spa, children's wading pool and the Seaside Grille were installed on the lawn next to the veranda. A trellis-covered wall adorned with seashells shaded the area.

According to George Mitchell, the exterior work alone cost approximately $4 million. While it was being completed, the design team studied old photographs and researched historical documents to mimic original interior colors, finishes and details of the lobby and foyer, both of which were expanded to their original size.

Plaster crown moldings in the 1911 Reading and Writing Room areas were restored, and the rooms were repurposed into meeting spaces.

During a previous renovation, the windows of the Music Room, or Grecian Room, were covered with drywall. This was removed during the Mitchell restoration process. Greek goddess figureheads were also uncovered above the doorways and were refurbished. The distinctive, original arched tops of the large loggia windows were also reopened, having been covered with plaster for decades.

Grand Heritage Hotels International took over management of the Hotel Galvez in August 1966, with the Mitchells retaining ownership.

In 2001, the Mitchells' historic preservation efforts throughout Galveston were honored when they received the National Trust for Historic Preservation's highest honor, the Louise du Pont Crowninshield Award.

Hotel Galvez became a member of Historic Hotels of America, a consortium sponsored by the National Trust for Historic Preservation, in 2002.

Sheridan Mitchell Lorenz, the couple's daughter, supervised a second renovation in 2005. The heavy drapes were removed from lobby windows, restoring an unobstructed view of the Gulf.

The basement area was remodeled, fabrics and carpets updated and an Oleander Garden installed in honor of her father and his love of the island. Due to its elegance and intimacy, the garden is a favorite wedding spot in Galveston.

Preservationists George P. and Cynthia Woods Mitchell.

Hotel Galvez loggia, viewing from west to east, 2000. *Author's collection.*

Enclosed Terrace dining area, 2000. *Author's collection.*

After three years in the planning stage, the spa at the Hotel Galvez opened its doors in March 2008. The nearly ten-thousand-square-foot Mediterranean-inspired facilities included nine treatment rooms, a salon and a fitness center on the hotel's lower level.

Hurricane Ike, a category 2 storm, arrived just before 2:00 a.m. on September 13, 2008, bringing a category 5 storm surge. Hotel Galvez lost roof tiles and had two feet of water in the lower level, including in its new spa, fitness center, sales offices, laundry facility and employee break area.

Numerous Galveston buildings sustained worse damage, and the Mitchells rallied to help, including repairing the portion of the Strand their company owned.

In July 2009, the fully restored spa reopened, and the Galvez could again invite guests to enjoy relaxing treatments and the Meditation Garden.

The Spirit of Galveston Award was presented to George and Cynthia Mitchell in 2009 to recognize the vital role they played in the renaissance of the historic downtown district.

The Queen of the Gulf's long-awaited one-hundred-year anniversary arrived in 2011. Centennial events occurred throughout the year and included a Spanish cultural evening on the birthday of Bernardo de Gálvez, a mass wedding vow renewal on the lawn for former guests who were married at the hotel and outdoor concerts.

The hotel was now a Wyndham Grand® Hotel. An $11 million update and renovation by the Mitchells took place to have the hotel looking its best for the big day. Each of the guest rooms and suites were redecorated with plush furnishings, flat-screen televisions and new bedding and drapes. The rooms also featured nature-inspired prints by artist Kayla Mitchell, the Mitchells' granddaughter.

The large, arched windows of the hotel were restored to their original grandeur, replacing the modern fixed-glass style. The operable, divided light windows were more in line with the hotel's original appearance.

An outdoor space used for a valet parking lot was redesigned into a landscaped green space called Centennial Green, just outside of the Music Hall. Resembling a park that existed when the hotel opened in 1911, it had a pergola and four delightful fountains.

On centennial day, Saturday, June 11, the community was invited to visit the new Hall of History on the Galvez's lower level, take self-guided tours of the hotel with a booklet provided by the Galvez and enjoy an assortment of family activities. Artist Gabrielle McNeese was on hand to sign the official

Current view of west entrance and entrance to Hotel Galvez spa. *Photo by author.*

Hotel Galvez one-hundredth anniversary commemorative Christmas ornament. *Author's collection.*

Hotel Galvez centennial poster she designed. The day culminated in a spectacular fireworks show over the Gulf of Mexico.

Mitchell Properties sold the Hotel Galvez and the Tremont House to a Texas-based hospitality, management and investment group in 2020. The Queen's next chapter is set to begin.

26

MR. BOBBY

Legendary Galvez Ambassador

In 2019, the Galvez and its visitors lost a beloved fixture: Bobby Lee Hilton, who was guest ambassador and resident historian for the hotel. Known affectionately by everyone as "Mr. Bobby," the gentle-spoken treasure seemed to know every corner and story associated with the Galvez throughout its history and was there to witness many of them.

The dapper, smiling gentleman with the gentle voice greeted guests and gave tours at the hotel for decades, sharing his encyclopedic knowledge of both official and unofficial stories surrounding the famous property, right down to where ghosts might dwell.

Below his name on his badge were the letters "B.O.I.," which stood for "born on the island," a designation that locals consider a point of honor.

Born in Galveston in 1933, Hilton first worked for the hotel as a busboy while attending Central High School, as did many of his classmates. The school and teachers allowed the students to work at the hotel at lunchtime and then return to campus for afternoon classes before returning for an evening shift.

His first job was pouring coffee and bussing tables in the restaurant and at banquets. Coffee cost a nickel when he began.

When he was a freshman in high school in 1949, General Dwight D. Eisenhower attended a banquet in the Marine Room of the Hotel Galvez, where 1,800 Galvestonians had gathered to hear him speak.

The nervous young Hilton was given the task of serving coffee at the special event. He often related the story of how his hands were shaking as he poured the general's cup of coffee. The dignitary noticed and softly encouraged Hilton to take his time, saying that he was doing a good job. Those words of kindness made a huge impression on the young man, who, luckily, proceeded to pour the drink without spilling a drop.

In addition to working at the Galvez and keeping up with his schoolwork, Hilton was a star player on his school's football team, earning a full scholarship to Texas Southern University.

After graduating college in 1956, he joined the army, where he served as a medic and was a quarterback for the Army Rangers football team in Alaska.

After his military service, Hilton worked in sales and management in the beer industry for thirty years, eventually becoming the Gulf Coast Regional District manager for Galveston's Falstaff Brewery, Schlitz Brewery and Stroh Brewing Company.

In 1993, at age fifty-nine, Hilton retired from the industry. But he had no intention of slowing down. He returned to the Galvez as lead waiter and bartender for special events, decades after he first worked at the hotel.

The Galvez added a Hall of History on the lower level in 2011. The obvious choice to serve as its tour guide was Hilton, who had become known for telling engaging stories about the history of the property. He was given the title "Guest Ambassador." His favorite part of his job as ambassador was

Linen postcard of the Hotel Galvez, circa 1935. *Author's collection.*

visiting with people and sharing stories of his beloved island and the hotel that became his second home.

Hilton had hundreds of stories about working at the hotel during the era of the "Free State of Galveston," his encounters with famous guests and how the hotel's past intertwined with bathing beauty pageants, gamblers, bootleggers, dignitaries, war heroes, celebrities and more. His gift for storytelling helped guests realize they were standing where history occurred. They came back repeatedly to experience his tours, which were never the same twice.

Over the years, Bobby and his tours were featured in television shows, news reports, magazines and newspapers, but he always remained humble about the attention he received, taking joy instead in the opportunity to share his stories.

When guests asked how long he had been at the Galvez, Bobby would laugh and tell them he came with the woodwork.

Bobby Lee Hilton passed away October 7, 2019, at the age of eighty-six, leaving his wife of sixty-five years, children, grandchildren, great-grandchildren, great-great-great-grandchildren and a community who loved to remember his stories.

Mr. Bobby has become part of the fabric of the history of the hotel he loved so dearly.

27

GHOSTLY GUESTS

As visitors walk the halls of the historic Hotel Galvez, they are never quite alone. Spirits of those whose paths have brought them to the historic grounds seem to want to remain in the beautiful hotel as much as present-day guests do.

From the very opening of the Galvez, there have been stories of spirits of people who haunted the land before the hotel was even built. One was even reportedly captured in an original press photo taken in 1911. An enlargement of the picture hangs in the west loggia of the hotel, where visitors can look at it and decide for themselves just what the anomaly might be. Many claim to clearly see the ghost of a gentleman standing in front of a French door, politely tipping his bowler hat.

Other spirits-in-residence that seem to predate the building itself are said to be those who were lost in the 1900 Storm. The most famous of these is Sister Katherine, a nun from St. Mary's Orphan Asylum, which was located just down the beach. During the height of the hurricane, the brave sisters of the orphanage lashed children to themselves in an effort to keep them from washing away. Tragically, all of the nuns and children who they clung to were drowned. The bodies of Sister Katherine and her wards, still tied together, were found on the shore in front of where the hotel now stands. As with so many storm victims, they were buried where they were found.

Witnesses have claimed to see the figure of a nun in a long, dark habit protectively pacing the southern lawn of the hotel and looking out to sea whenever a major storm approaches the coast. Occasionally, she waves a warning to anyone walking along the beach. The dedicated sister continues to keep watch over the playful spirits of the children, to whom many of the ghostly pranks in the hotel are credited.

Room showers and lights turn off and on, toilets flush and televisions flicker. These modern luxuries would surely be tempting novelties to children from 1900. Ethereal visions of children from the hurricane seem to have joined with those from other eras in transforming the grand hotel into their own playground.

The ghost of a young girl bouncing a red ball has been seen multiple times through the years by guests, staff and workmen. The ball makes no sound as it bounces off the hard floor, and her form seems to slowly fade as she walks, uninterested in those who watch her. She is sometimes seen on the second floor as well, with her appearance beginning with a small white light before developing into an apparition.

Coincidently—or not—workers during a reconstruction project often reported seeing a girl with a red ball standing in the basement.

A female bartender once heard the voice of a small boy crying from right behind her, calling out for his mother. She quickly turned around, and the crying immediately stopped. There was no one there.

High-pitched children's laughs are heard as doors slam shut, and the sound of running feet echo up and down the hallways on the fifth floor. Curious guests open their doors, ready to scold unruly youngsters, only to see empty hallways.

Certain spirits seem to appear quite clearly to guests, who can describe their appearance in detail. One of these is a little girl about three feet tall who plays just outside the door to the spa. Her blond pigtails are tied with ribbon, and she is wearing a white dress with black "Mary Jane" shoes, a popular style in the early twentieth century. She has been heard to whisper the words "ice cream" into the ears of passersby. This can be explained by the fact that the hotel soda fountain and ice-cream parlor used to be where the spa is now located.

She might also be one of the tiny ghosts that leave child-sized handprints along the bottom of the glass spa door. Employees confirm that, though they may wipe them off multiple times a day and never see children in the area, the small prints quickly reappear.

A teenage girl in a violet-sprigged organdy dress with a violet sash quietly smiles as she rides the elevator. Her blond hair is tied with a violet bow, and she wears high-button shoes that would have been fashionable about the

Children standing on riprap near seawall in front of Hotel Galvez, circa 1911.

same time the hotel held its opening. Perhaps she once stayed here with her parents and has returned to relive happy memories.

The spirits of children aren't the only ones who call the Galvez home. Several specters of Victorian ladies in elegant clothing have been sighted as well. Groups of ladies from this era have been seen wandering the Music Room and sitting in the ballroom as if attending social gatherings. Even when the specters aren't visible, distinct cold spots can sometimes be felt in the Terrace Ballroom. Whispered conversations in the Music Room between unseen confidants cease immediately when someone opens the door to investigate.

Guests who expect a moment of privacy in the ground-floor restrooms near the Music Hall might be surprised to be joined by invisible company. The ladies' room seems to exhibit the most activity, with toilets flushing by themselves, water in the sinks turning on unassisted, handles of stalls rattling, stall doors slamming and, occasionally, heavy breathing inside one of the stalls. Though most of these occurrences seem mischievous, witnesses have also experienced what they describe as feeling like a sudden drop in air pressure, making breathing difficult before hearing the sobs of a woman.

While the men's room seems quieter, an elderly man who stares back from the mirror with a mournful expression can make it just as unsettling.

The most famous ghost of the Hotel Galvez is called Audra, also known as the Lovelorn Bride. Her story is classically tragic, in the style of Romeo and Juliet. Audra was engaged to a mariner who sailed out of the Port of Galveston. In the mid-1950s, she checked into Room 501 at the Hotel Galvez to await his return, after which they planned to be married.

Each day, she would walk down the hall of the fifth floor, take an elevator to the eighth and then climb a narrow ladder leading to one of the four turrets atop the hotel. Sitting inside the shelter of the hexagonal turret, she would watch through an opening for his ship to return.

When Audra received the news that her lover's ship had gone down in a storm with all hands on deck, she refused to abandon hope. She kept her vigil of returning to the turret to watch for him, but after several days, the heartbroken bride-to-be accepted that she would never see him again. In despair, she hanged herself in the west turret, where she had last seen his ship sail out to sea.

Color postcard of the Hotel Galvez, circa 1950.

As if her story was not tragic enough, a few days after her death, her fiancée came looking for her at the hotel. It seems that he had been rescued by a passing ship during the storm.

To this day, because of the reported paranormal events that Audra causes in Room 501, it is the most requested room at the hotel, though she doesn't always want company. Most visitors simply feel uncomfortable, but others have more memorable encounters.

Shortly after her death, people began reporting light coming from the tower at night, where no electricity existed at the time.

The hotel and staff have collected countless accounts of ghostly experiences in the room over the years in the room that has been visited by numerous news and film crews.

When Audra isn't feeling social, no key will work to open the door to her room. In recent years, one guest returned a problematic, electronic key to the front desk and asked for the assistance of the desk clerk. When the key was scanned to check for a room code, the display read, "Expired 1955."

The phone in 501 has been known to repeatedly ring at night, yet the switchboard reports no calls were received at the time.

Guests have felt the pressure of something invisible sitting on the bed beside them or heard a disembodied voice whisper their name from behind.

Workers and guests alike have heard footsteps or seen the misty form of a woman retracing Audra's steps down the halls of the fifth floor, hearing soft whimpering sobs as she nears the elevators. Sometimes, they detect the smell of gardenias, reportedly a favorite perfume of the young girl. The same scent sometimes wafts through the lobby, leading employees to believe that Audra doesn't confine herself to one floor.

In addition to Audra and the children who roam the fifth floor, scratching sounds and a woman's voice have been reported in rooms 500, 501 and 503. If guests are faint of heart, they may want to consider any other floor.

An unnerving bit of decor at the Galvez has kept a watchful eye on the occurrences of the hotel since it opened. The portrait of the hotel's namesake, Bernardo de Gálvez, hangs in the west foyer at the end of a corridor. Many visitors who approach it begin to feel uneasy even before seeing it up close. Legend has it that the extremely white eyes of the painting follow guests as they walk by. Because of its reputation, visitors often attempt to photograph the painting but end up with a skull-shaped glare where the face should appear in the photo. Staffers insist that this can be avoided by asking the infamous portrait's permission before a photo is taken. After all, what can a polite gesture hurt?

One guest told the front desk as he was checking out that loose change he had tossed onto the desk in his room before going to bed had been neatly sorted and stacked by the time he awoke.

People who have worked at the Galvez in the last century sometimes seem to continue their responsibilities of looking after the hotel, even after they pass away. In the days after Hurricane Ike struck the island in 2008, a few members of the staff lived at the hotel while their own homes were being repaired. Several of them saw a woman dressed in an old-fashioned maid uniform and a man walking through guest rooms as if to inspect them before disappearing.

The Hotel Galvez and its staff fully embrace the reported hauntings on the property, gladly answering questions and sharing experiences they have had themselves.

A longtime switchboard operator became frustrated one night when she was repeatedly called from Room 409 one evening, but she could get no response when she dialed the room back. Worried that someone might have needed assistance, she sent a staff member up to the room to check. When the shaken man returned, he reported that not only was no one checked into that room, but it also was being renovated and had no furniture or phone.

A repairman was called to Room 503 to fix a television set that wasn't functioning. When he pulled the electrical cord out of the TV, leaving it with no power, it suddenly came on. Having experience with the ghostly occurrences at the hotel, he didn't hesitate before uttering, "Enjoy yourself!" before hurriedly leaving the room.

In the lobby, a female concierge once heard a man's voice whisper into her ear, "We like you." From that point on, she felt a special affinity with the Galvez ghosts, knowing she had their approval.

Those who work alongside the spirits have also witnessed dishes breaking by themselves, candles extinguishing without a breeze and glasses flying off tables when no one is near.

Of course, these types of events are far less messy than what has taken place in the wine cellar. During one incident, wine bottles fell out of perfectly balanced, horizontal racks when no one was in the room. Another time, an entire shelf of wine bottles exploded. When the staff had cleaned up the disarray and placed new bottles in the racks, they exploded as well.

The good news for anyone who is hesitant about sharing space with the possibility of ghosts is that those that reside at the Galvez all seem to be quite playful, if a bit mischievous. The one exception, of course, is the ominous presence of a man who stands in a corner of the hotel's laundry room in the

A busy day on the seawall with automobiles, bicycles, horse-drawn carriages and pedestrians, circa 1916. *Author's collection.*

basement. It's possible that this is the same entity that silently stands by the pool during the night.

Ghosts have become such a part of the Hotel Galvez that the current concierge, Melissa Hall, now leads ghost tours of the property year-round. The tours end with a private dinner and drinks on the property so that attendees can compare experiences and enjoy the exquisite hotel that so many spirits call home.

INDEX

ABOUT THE AUTHOR

Kathleen Maca is a writer, speaker and photographer with a lifelong love of tales from the past. She regularly writes magazine features, sharing stories about the history of people and places in Texas. Her blog *Tales from Texas* at www.kathleenmaca.com shares travel ideas around the Lone Star State.

A member of the Texas Chapter of the Association for Gravestone Studies, her work with historic cemeteries earned the National Society Daughters of the American Revolution Historic Preservation Award in 2019.

Kathleen is a graduate of Sam Houston State University and the author of *Galveston's Broadway Cemeteries* and *Ghosts of Galveston*.